PREACHING ON
THE CRUCIFIXION

PREACHING ON THE CRUCIFIXION

D.W. CLEVERLEY FORD

MOWBRAY

Mowbray
A Cassell imprint
Wellington House
125 Strand
London WC2R 0BB

PO Box 605
Herndon
VA 290172

First published 1993

Reprinted 1997

British Library Cataloguing-in-Publication Data
A catalogue record for this book is available from the British Library.

Library of Congress Cataloging-in-Publication Data
Available from the Library of Congress.

ISBN 0-264-67282-8

Typeset by Colset Private Limited, Singapore
Printed and bound in Great Britain by
Biddles Ltd, Guildford and King's Lynn

CONTENTS

ACKNOWLEDGEMENTS

The publishers, Mowbray, gave me six months in which to write this book, so I am grateful to my wife for being patient with a preoccupied husband throughout that period; and to Miss B.L. Hodge for working hard to have my handwritten MS typed in time to meet this deadline.

D.W. Cleverley Ford
Lingfield 1992

INTRODUCTION

Like the preceding books in this series, this one also is written for non-specialists, and while it may serve as a resource book for those who are called to preach it is by no means limited to this use. It seeks to open up in non-technical language what every Christian knows is basic in the Christian faith, namely, the crucifixion, so basic that any person, any place, almost any article stamped with the cross is to some degree Christian. Has some archaeological site been unearthed, even some household utensil been discovered, if marked with the cross, it is at once recognized as evidence in that place of Christian faith.

We have, however, grown used to it. That is our trouble, we take it for granted. It is not unlike the Eiffel Tower, the erection and strangeness of which barely arouses the interest of more than a minority of people although it dominates the Parisian skyline. Similarly the cross. Certainly we see it. We can't help seeing it. It is the focal point in our churches. We have gilded it, flanked it with flowers, woven it on garments, carried it about and on occasions venerated it. But why? The cross is an ugly thing. It stands for something unbelievably brutal. What permanent message can this instrument of torture possibly have for mankind in general? What in particular can modern man see there? These are the kind of questions I have tried to keep in mind in writing this book.

I have not launched at the outset into theological interpretations of the cross listing theories of the atonement with scholarly names attached. This is not the way to preach the crucified Christ to people hectically busy in the restless world of today; nor is to treat it as essentially a spiritual way of life. It is not. First of all the cross of Christ is a thing; it stood as a ghastly object on a repulsive historical site. And this is how the New Testament introduces it, not as a doctrine. This comes later, it must come, it comes in the epistles, but in the gospels there are only hints. What we are given at the outset is the *story of the crucifixion*, detailed, restrained and moving. More precisely we are provided with four complementary accounts of the death of the Incarnate Christ whom through these writings it is possible to some extent to know. It is this Jesus we must see before we venture on theories.

The story evokes questions both historical and literary but the preacher must keep them in the margin. He must remember that he will not be convincing if he relies on intellect alone. He must tell the story with feeling. And when he has sat down, he has to face the question as to whether the whole point of the story is to cry aloud that identification with the poor, the outcast, the maimed and the broken is the supreme height of human virtue, marking out what should be the aim of all political and social programmes. Yes, but is it the whole point? Does not the crucifixion reach down to far deeper levels such as the human being's relation to God, the obvious flaw in human nature, our final destiny and the offence of death? Fundamental questions from which we may be tempted to hide but cannot escape. Was Christ really crucified to provide answers here? This is the ground on which we shall need to wrestle and from which we may be tempted to run. And who dares to stand up and preach Christ crucified in the face of such demanding questions? But preaching on the crucifixion there must be, for it is there that the very heart of the Christian gospel beats. There is no Christianity without it.

For me to list all the standard works on the atonement to which I am indebted would be tedious; so I will restrict myself to three recent publications which have stimulated my thinking on the subject and provided fresh insights:

Charles B. Coursar, *A Theology of the Cross: The Death of Jesus in the Pauline Letters* (Fortress Press, Minneapolis, 1990).

Vernon White, *Atonement and Incarnation: An Essay in Universalism and Particularity* (Cambridge University Press, 1991).

Barnabas Lindars SSF, *The Theology of the Letter to the Hebrews* (Cambridge University Press, 1991).

D.W.C.F.
1992

1

WHY JESUS WAS CRUCIFIED

*And when they came to the place which is called The Skull, there they
crucified him.*

LUKE 23.33 (RSV)

I am going to preach about the crucifixion. And you look at me with dismay. 'I suppose we must put up with this', your face is saying, 'after all this is the season of Lent, but thank God it only lasts some six weeks, then we can return to more uplifting subjects. Come to think of it, aren't there troubles enough in the modern world without harping on one ghastly event two thousand years ago? People are being tortured *now*. Ask Amnesty International. And who is there who isn't wearied with the news bulletins depressing us with a daily dose of dire calamities. Rarely anything cheerful! No, Mr Preacher, don't dwell on the crucifixion too long.'

I understand. I am by nature a cheerful person. I enjoy funny things as well as you, but I hope I am also a sensitive person. Life isn't all fun and games. Some stretches of the road are so rough they are painful to negotiate. And what lies at the end? This is the worry. Too often fear of the future brings people almost to breaking point. Yes, I am a preacher, but before that I am a priest and a pastor and have been for many years, which being the case I will laugh with you, but I will also cry with you if need be. A ministry with nothing to offer at the breaking points of human experience is not a proper ministry. But it reaches down not to wallow in the gloom but to let in shafts of light, and life, and perhaps in time even some laughter. This is what the crucifixion was for, is for. So please do not react with dismay when I announce that I intend preaching about it, not even when I tell you that I shall need more than one sermon to open up the subject. I shall not be gloomy and I shall not be unpractical. I care for people, not theories. And if we do not come to the end of the course with uplifted hearts I shall have failed.

1

1 WHY JESUS WAS CRUCIFIED

Now the crucifixion happened. I return to the text. 'When they came to the place which is called The Skull, there they crucified him.' There is nothing speculative about it. It stands as a brutal fact of history but it cannot be shut up in history because it tells of the crucifixion of Christ. Therefore it speaks to men and women of all time and not only of tragedy. I was astonished and impressed to see on the television screen at the time of the failed coup in Moscow in August 1991 a huge white wooden cross openly being carried at the funeral of the three young men who lost their lives in the struggle for freedom. Why display this if it is merely a commemoration of an historical event two thousand years ago? Why bring it to bear on a contemporary situation unless it is reckoned to have something to say now? There must be a word of the cross, and it is for our welfare to listen to what that word is. So we preach it and not only in Lent.

We must not however gloss over the historical event. We must begin there. If we lose this we lose all. Not by accident is it that all four gospels in the New Testament provide extended descriptions of the crucifixion as of no other event in the story of Jesus, not even the resurrection, and certainly not the nativity. The crucifixion is the pivot on which the whole New Testament turns including the writings other than the four gospels.

But why was Jesus crucified? Modern man for ever seeking scientific causes for events is bound to ask this question long before considering theological answers, if ever he comes round to them. The New Testament however has little interest in scientific and historical causation. It tells the story of the crucifixion in the gospels and works out the implications for mankind in the epistles. Even so the question will not go away. Why was Jesus crucified? No one suffered this fate for nothing. What had Jesus done? What had he said? Had he offended the Jews? Did the Romans see him as a threat to political stability? Did Jesus, as has been suggested, deliberately act and speak provocatively so as to 'paint himself into a corner' and thus encourage martyrdom by which he would gain widespread influence? This is like asking if Jesus aimed to be crucified.

Let us look at the situation a little more closely. That Jesus' words and deeds did offend the Jewish hierarchy of his time is clear. For one thing he broke the Sabbath, on occasions deliberately, by healing the sick on that day. This was unpardonable because the Jews did not merely keep the Sabbath, the Sabbath kept the Jewish people together as a distinctive nation. Jesus was seen therefore as a national affront. Moreoever he did not scorn to interpret on his own authority the sacrosanct law of Moses. Worse still, he claimed to forgive sins, which appeared as near blasphemy as could possibly be.

2 THE PROBLEMS FOR THE AUTHORITIES

All this stirred the common people. They were ready, or half ready, to hail him as their leader. This was the trouble. The Jewish hierarchy sensed danger, danger not least to the fragile peace between the Jewish people and the Roman occupying power. On account of Jesus there might break out a movement of popular unrest which the Romans would be quick to crush. Desperate action was therefore called for. If Jesus could not be muzzled or banished he must be killed. But how? This was the tantalizing yet urgent question that clamoured for decisive action.

Decisive action however was not easy. If the hierarchy proceeded forthwith to arrest Jesus, supposing they could carry it out secretly, there would probably result a popular uprising, the very situation they were anxious to avoid. And in any case had they the authority under the Roman occupation to carry out the death penalty? And suppose they had, stoning to death would be the Jewish method, not crucifixion which was a Roman device. Either way the hierarchy would have a martyr on their hands. All in all they were in desperate straits what to do with Jesus. Of this however they were convinced, somehow he must be discredited, not simply killed—discredited in the eyes of the Jewish public. But how? That was the problem.

And then a way out appeared. Deuteronomy 21.22, 23 reads 'And if a man has committed a crime punishable by death and he is put to death, and you hang him on a tree, his body shall not remain all night upon the tree, but you shall bury him the same day, for *a hanged man is accursed by God*'. This was it, Jesus must be hanged upon a tree, he must be crucified, not stoned. He must be exhibited on a cross of wood, then all would know he was cursed by God, he was a cursed man.

Yet still an obstacle remained. The plan required the co-operation of the Roman Governor. He alone was responsible for crucifixions. This was Pontius Pilate. But would he co-operate? He was not interested in religious questions. Jesus would have to be presented to him as a political danger without which there was little likelihood of his falling in with the hierarchy's plans. So Jesus was presented to Pilate as a rival king to Caesar. And when Pilate demurred for Jesus did not look like a rival king to the Roman emperor they suggested that he, Pilate, would incur the emperor's displeasure if he did not crush forthwith a potential rival. This was not a complaint Pilate wished to be transmitted to Rome, and so with a bad conscience he gave way. A piece of wood was inscribed with the words 'Jesus the King of the Jews' (Pilate's wry joke against the Jews) and he, Jesus, was made to carry it or it was carried before him to the place of crucifixion and nailed up over his cross. So the hierarchy had the grim satisfaction of seeing him hanging on a tree as one cursed of God. And all the people crowding round the crucifixion would see Jesus as a man cursed of God and so thoroughly discredited. The end had been achieved. The chief priests were satisfied. They could return home their minds at ease. An ugly political crisis had been averted.

3 THE MESSAGE OF THE CRUCIFIXION

And now someone listening to all this, even if following the line of thought, is despairing of remaining attentive if the preaching on the crucifixion that is promised is set to proceed in this fashion of historical enquiry. What can there be in this for ordinary people like ourselves? So let me end by bringing it to the point where St Paul brought it in 1 Corinthians 15.3, 'For I delivered unto you that which I also received, how that Christ died *for our sins* according to the scriptures'. A housewife heard the message from an ordinary church pulpit. Her husband had been carried off in a matter of four days by the influenza epidemic of 1918 and for some years she had struggled as a widow bringing up her two boys. What would not let her mind rest was the consciousness that she had not perhaps been all she might have been in relation to the man she had lost. Unexpectedly, however, as the outcome of a chance invitation over her garden wall she attended a church where she heard this preaching, 'Christ died for our sins according to the Scriptures'. She reached out to grasp the message and the miracle happened, not all at once, but gradually she was released of her burden and gave herself to the upbringing of her two boys in a new-found freedom. Had you tried to convince her that the crucifixion had nothing to say to her you would have failed, she knew better. This is a true story. That woman was my mother.

2

JESUS FORESAW HIS CRUCIFIXION

*And he began to teach them that the Son of man must suffer many
things, and be rejected by the elders and the chief priests and the scribes,
and be killed, and after three days rise again. And he said this plainly.*

MARK 8.31–32 (RSV)

Not long ago I heard of a man who, as we say, 'smoked like a chimney'.
There was never a quarter of an hour in the day when a cigarette was not
dangling from his mouth. Considering how he suffered from a lung complaint anyway it might have been thought that he would exercise some
restraint, if not desist from smoking altogether. But no, he went on and
on, so that not surprisingly those who knew him began to wonder if per-
chance he might be harbouring a secret death wish.

Now circumstances do exist when a longing to die is understandable.
It is possible to become so enfeebled by old age that the normal instinct to
cling on to life dies. And long imprisonment, torture or fear of a public
trial for a crime guiltily committed can rub out the will to live. Misery
can lead to suicide. None of this however is normal. It is natural to shun
death, even to avoid thinking about it, let alone talking about it. People
with a death wish are broken people. At best we can only feel desperately
sorry for them.

1 THREE INTERPRETATIONS OF THE CRUCIFIXION

So I raise my question. Did Jesus come into the world in order con-
sciously to die? This is not a silly question when you consider the basic
Christian belief that his death constituted his ministry. Did he not at the
Last Supper break bread and pour out wine, saying 'This is my body, this
is my blood which is shed for you and for many for the remission of sins'?
Is not Christ's death as Christ's ministry for us impressed on us at every
service of Holy Communion, the central act of Christian worship? Christ

5

died *for us*. So did Jesus come into the world in order to die? And if he did, was death in his mind, we might say, *on* his mind all the days of his life? If so, all I can say is 'Poor little boy, poor young man in and around the home, poor family having to live with such a person perpetually death-conscious'. No, I cannot believe that all his life Jesus was looking ahead to dying. Were this so he would have been abnormal, not a real, whole and wholesome person. What is more such deformity would involve a denial of the incarnation. Jesus' humanity was perfect. He was perfect man, not warped, not broken, not stunted, not bound, but free. Jesus was alive. The New Testament is categorical. 'In him was life, and the life was the light of men' (John 1.4 RSV). Surely then we can be emphatic about his crucifixion. This is not what he wanted. Death was not what he dwelt on as he walked about in Galilee and Judaea.

Let us think again. Must we say then that the crucifixion overtook Jesus? Must we say that he was trapped by the crucifixion, in which case his was a supreme case of innocence being snared by powers he was unable either to avoid or resist? In this case what the crucifixion stands to cry aloud is the tragic nature of our human existence. Even Jesus was overtaken by it just as some men and women are cut off in the prime of life by accident or illness through no fault of their own. So the crucifixion is set before us as a garish portrayal of misfortune, the proper reaction to which must be pity. Poor Jesus! Poor many a man and woman! This makes Good Friday a day for weeping forgetting that on the way to the crucifixion site Jesus said to the women shedding tears as they watched this striking man stumble on the road 'Weep not for me, but weep for yourselves and your children'. Granted, to feel no sadness at all at this sight would be grossly insensitive but to be sorry for Jesus as one more illustration of the harshness of life is surely to miss what the crucifixion is about.

And now a third suggestion. Did Jesus perhaps begin his ministry in the fullness of hope that through the power of his words, the effectiveness of his healings and the arresting presence of his personality he would inaugurate the Kingdom of God in Galilee and Judaea? But he was mistaken. His way was blocked. Opponents reared their heads and reacted to his goodness with hate. But the world is like that. The greater the good the more fiercely do some people attack it. But is this the correct interpretation? Was Jesus as ignorant as this of the world in which he lived? Had he learned nothing in his thirty years in the narrowness of Nazareth including years working and trading as a carpenter? Was Jesus really a starry-eyed religious enthusiast? Was he a poor innocent? And if we reject this as too simplistic an interpretation are we prepared for a more subtle version of it and assert that he began his ministry with high hopes but when he saw the storm clouds gathering he altered his tactics and went for the role of a martyr, even if it involved crucifixion, as likely to produce the more powerful and lasting impression on people? On these terms the ministry of Jesus was not based on principle, it was an adjusted one, adjusted to circumstances.

2 THE CHRIST MUST SUFFER

The trouble with all three interpretations of the crucifixion is that they leave us with a Christ who is only one of us, a fellow sufferer in the human predicament which in greater degree or lesser degree we all experience. We may pity him, we may admire him but we are left with no one before whom to bow the knee and worship, certainly not on Good Friday. The death of Jesus had to be *a positive and willing sacrifice* to what he saw was most likely to come to him. He was not conscripted to the cross by circumstances or any other power, nor did he court it but he walked willingly to what came with wide open eyes.

And now it is up to me as a preacher to establish what I am saying. So my text from Mark 8.31, 32 (RSV). 'And he (Jesus) began to teach them that the Son of man must suffer many things, and be rejected by the elders and the chief priests and the scribes, and be killed, and after three days rise again. And he said this plainly.'

For weeks, months, even a year or two Jesus had been conducting his ministry far and wide throughout the country teaching, healing, yes, and puzzling everyone who this could be to possess such powers. Even the twelve disciples were perplexed. Then at last there came a day when journeying with them in the region of Caesarea Philippi to the north of Galilee, impressive by reason of Mount Hermon towering nine thousand feet above them, he asked 'Who do people say I am?' and then, 'Who do you say I am?' The stunned silence could be felt. No doubt disconcerted they searched each other's faces wondering which of them possessed the courage and conviction to reply. Then Peter took the plunge. 'You are the Christ.' Was there a gasp? The turning point in the ministry had come. St Mark in his gospel stresses the occasion (8.31): 'Then it was that he began (note the word 'began') to teach them that the Son of man must suffer many things, and be rejected by the elders and the chief priests and the scribes, and be killed, and after three days rise again'. Note the word 'must'. Jesus pointed to the necessity of his death.

Perhaps we need to pause here. Can we really believe, knowing as we do the limitations of his mind because he really was truly man, can we really accept *as it stands* this detailed forecasting of what was to take place? Must we not say that this is Mark's wording, not Jesus' actual words, telling the story as it was frequently told in the early Church preaching? and that the reference to rising again after three days is taken from Hosea 6.1 in the Old Testament? Possibly, but this does not alter the fact that the journey to Caesarea Philippi was the time and place when Jesus began to divulge to his disciples what he had known for a long time and now had come to see plainly that inevitably he would be deliberately killed.

I want to emphasize the phrase 'come to see'. Jesus came to see *as his ministry developed* that it would involve a violent death. He did not want it, he did not court it, he certainly had no death wish all his days, but when he saw even from early on what his ministry involved he did not attempt to escape it. Let me spell this out.

About the age of thirty Jesus left his home in Nazareth. No longer would he be the village carpenter, he would begin a public ministry of teaching and healing. His first step was to make his way to the Jordan river to line up with the motley mixture of penitents queueing up for baptism by one called John who looked for all the world like an Old Testament prophet, which in fact he was, the last of them. A wave of religious repentance was sweeping the land. Like all the prophets John the Baptist paid for his outspokenness. Herod Antipas, the puppet king of the region, had him beheaded in Fort Machaerus down by the Dead Sea. Jesus, having been baptized himself and anointed with the Spirit of God, read John's murder as the signal for him to follow on and begin his dynamic ministry in Galilee. Could he have been in any doubt what would befall him too? But he kept his secret to himself till the time came at Caesarea Philippi when he put the great question to his disciples— 'Who do you say I am?' And when Peter dared to declare his verdict 'You are the Christ' Jesus insisted that he was not to be thought of as Messiah apart from death. He was not a conquering Christ, he was a suffering Christ, suffering was an essential part of his ministry.

Peter objected in no uncertain terms. He even took it upon himself to rebuke Jesus: 'God forbid, Lord! This shall never happen to you' (Matthew 16.22). The rebuke he received in return was biting. 'Get behind me, Satan! You are a hindrance to me, for you are not on the side of God, but of men.'

8

3 NO CHRISTIANITY WITHOUT THE CROSS

Let me bring this out of past history into our own thinking and way of thinking. We, as with Peter, would like to have Christ without his crucifixion. We would like to have Christianity without the cross. We would like to have Jesus as a supreme teacher. We would like the Sermon on the Mount to be paramount. We would like Christianity to be the way of successful living, the way of wisdom, the way of psychological and physical well-being. And there is something in these interpretations. Those who know North America well and are entitled to speak on this tell us that generally speaking the Christian message is presented as the way to achieve personal integration and mastery, not least collectively to build up the nation. The cross is an embarrassment.

Recently in a book entitled *A Theology of the Cross* by Charles B. Cousar I read how in a BBC series of programmes depicting various aspects of religious life the success story of a popular American television preacher was sympathetically presented. The sumptuous church was shown and the crowds that came weekly to hear his positive and affirming sermons telling his hearers what they could achieve. 'And what do you think of Jesus?' asked the interviewer. He replied, 'He was the most successful religious figure of all time. He began in obscurity and today his followers outnumber those of any of the world's religions.' 'But I thought he ended up on a cross' said the interviewer. 'Oh no' came the answer. 'He was raised from the dead. The cross was something he had to endure as any successful person must endure hardships . . . He overcame the cross and put all that behind him.'

Let me be honest. We like this. It appeals to our desire to make a good thing of life. But is this view of the crucifixion true to the New Testament? Self-denial is embedded in the Christian way of life and it hurts. Immediately after this scripture in St Mark's gospel about the great confession at Caesarea Philippi Jesus is reported as saying to his disciples 'If any man would come after me, let him deny himself and take up his cross and follow me. For whoever would save his life will lose it; and whoever loses his life for my sake and the gospel's will save it.'

No, we cannot escape the cross. There is no Christianity without it. There is no Christianity without denial of self, and self-denial hurts.

3

THE BETRAYAL

Judas, then, received the bread and went out. It was night.

JOHN 13.30 (NEB)

Today I shall have to speak about Judas Iscariot. I put it this way because it simply is not possible to preach on the crucifixion in any comprehensive way without mentioning him. Not that I imply that there would have been no crucifixion without the betrayal of Christ by this man. By one means or another the priests in Jerusalem at the time would have found ways by which to rid themselves and their country of him whom they rated as a dangerous rival to themselves. What Judas did was to play into their hands and suddenly make possible the achievement of their nefarious purpose which every day that passed appeared to be beyond their grasp. They must have rubbed their hands in glee over Judas. He seemed almost too good to be true. And they had to pay almost nothing for his services when they might have been willing to surrender half their temple resources so dangerous did they count Jesus to be.

You won't, I hope, expect me even to attempt to suggest motives which prompted Judas to betray his Master. No one knows. What I can attempt, and should attempt is to tell the story of how he came to do what he did.

1 JUDAS THE MAN

First I have to say that Jesus chose Judas to be one of his twelve disciples, a member therefore of the trusted inner circle. His name, Iscariot, *Ish Kerioth*, may indicate that he hailed from Kerioth, a place east of the Jordan river; no one knows for certain. If so he was something of an outsider among the other disciples. Had he some special gift, something about him which attracted Jesus? Anyway he was appointed treasurer of the apostolic band and was trusted with money. Jesus had not chosen a traitor, Judas became a traitor. So the Greek of Luke 6.16. But when and why he became disaffected we do not know. He had certainly lived with Jesus like the rest of the chosen twelve, ate and drank with him, listened to his preaching and teaching and marvelled at his wonderful works. He must have seen in Jesus a leader of incomparable potentiality.

Not until a week before the crucifixion did the secret of his disaffection begin to show up and that only slightly. Jesus was present at a supper in the house at Bethany of Simon the leper, for a leper he once had been. Attention however came to be focused not on Simon but on the woman called Mary who displayed her gratitude to Jesus by anointing him with exceedingly costly perfume, openly. Judas, the treasurer (and some reckoned the dishonest treasurer), showed his disgust by voicing the amount of money for which the perfume might have been sold and the proceeds distributed to the poor. What really riled him however was the preoccupation on the part of Jesus with his own death and burial for which he declared this anointing was a fitting preparation. Did Judas then read this as sheer defeatism marking out Jesus as unfit for triumphant leadership? In order to win, a man must believe that he will win, not harp on his death.

Whether or not this was the precise occasion when Judas wrote off Jesus as worth his allegiance, certainly it was soon after this supper that he made his way to the priests actually in council at that time discussing how to apprehend Jesus. Clearly Judas had put his finger on who were the real enemies of his Master. He bargained with them in return for the information he would provide as to how they might capture Jesus safely. Ready money was on the table and Judas went away with the dirty silver coins tucked in his girdle to rejoin Jesus and the rest of the apostles all the time scheming in his mind how to deliver up his Master without drawing a crowd. Then events took an unexpected turn.

2 THE ACT OF BETRAYAL

Jesus knowing that his life was in danger kept his twelve disciples, including Judas, in ignorance as to where he would observe the forthcoming Passover festival. He made secret arrangements himself without their knowledge or assistance. Absolutely no one must be told, least of all Judas. So the disciples found themselves at the last moment actually alone with Jesus in an upper room in Jerusalem with only one exit. It was after dark. Was this the opportunity for which Judas was waiting? If he summoned the priests to make an arrest at once would not Jesus and the whole apostolic band be 'in the bag' without anyone in Jerusalem being alerted? But how was the message to the priests to be conveyed?

Judas had to wait. The proceedings in the upper room must have seemed interminable but at last all assembled for the meal, each of the thirteen present reclining at table on his left elbow according to custom, leaving free the right hand to partake of the food and drink. Jesus was the host. To his right was John, to his left possibly Peter, but more likely Judas, the treasurer. Jesus all at once astonished all present by announcing that one of them would betray him. And when in their horror they enquired of him who it could be Peter nodded to John closest to Jesus and said 'Ask who it is he means', which leaning back he did: 'Lord, who is it?' Then came the reply, 'It is the man to whom I give this piece of bread when I have dipped it in the dish'. This was the customary way of signalling out an honoured guest. It was Judas's last chance to recover his loyalty. He did not grasp it. Jesus saw that he did not grasp it. Then he gave him the bread and said 'Do quickly what you have to do'. The others at the table, if they heard this, did not know what was meant. Judas received the bread from Jesus' hands, left the table, went to the door and opened it. Puzzled eyes followed him. They noticed how dark it was outside. Judas descended down the stairway. Not long after Jesus would pass through the same door out into the same darkness, but not before he had instituted the Eucharist for it was in this tense atmosphere of betrayal that this was done. Meanwhile Judas was panting on his way to inform the priests where they could apprehend Jesus. His scheme was working. Jesus had not announced to all present at the table that he, Judas, would betray him. Just as well for Judas, for there were two swords at least in that room that night and eleven strong men, enough to overpower any traitor who was identified. Jesus however did not give them the chance, he let Judas go. And when he saw him pass through the door out into the dark he knew his death was sealed and the time was short. This was what took place on the night before the crucifixion in an upper room in Jerusalem at what is called the Last Supper.

Judas met Jesus once more. He was at the head of a crowd with swords and clubs come from the chief priests, scribes and elders to arrest him in the garden of Gethsemane whither he had gone with his disciples after leaving the upper room. Lest the scheme founder at the last moment and the wrong man be taken Judas had given them a sign: 'The one I shall kiss is the man, seize him and lead him away safely'. As soon therefore as

Judas saw Jesus in the garden he hastened up to him and said 'Master' and kissed him. So Jesus was captured.

Contrary to what might be expected the New Testament nowhere dwells on Judas. He is consistently designated as the traitor wherever his name occurs but that is all. Reproaches are not heaped on his head nor is he held up as a supreme example of evil worthy of the direst fate. St Matthew briefly tells of his repentance, return of his dirty money to the chief priests and how he committed suicide, in what may be a later addition to the gospel; and the book of the Acts of the Apostles has a short note about a field in Jerusalem said to have been purchased with Judas's payment for the betrayal. The New Testament does not satisfy our curiosity about Judas or his destiny. The crucifixion dominates all and the traitor only comes into the story in so far as is necessary to explain what happened.

3 THE CONTROL OF EVENTS

Let us think about this. Jesus knew from the outset of his ministry that it would be fraught with danger. Enemies did not in fact take long to appear bending their minds and energies to bring him down. He knew and in consequence was forced before long to conceal his whereabouts from time to time and even to escape across the frontier for safety. Clearly he did not intend that his violent death, which he foresaw, should be sprung upon him. He would determine the place and time. It would be Jerusalem when the Passover Festival was in progress and the sacrificial lambs being slain. So he kept the control of events in his hands to the very end of his life. Accordingly he took care not to be out and about in the streets of Jerusalem after dark during the Passover week, fair game for any assassin. His arrest would be brought about not by an outsider in the streets but by an insider, and he, Jesus, would actually tell the insider, the traitor, when to carry out the final act of treachery as events unfolded. 'Do quickly what you have to do' he said to Judas in the upper room at the Last Supper. Judas was not the master controller, on the contrary he was but the unwitting assistant in the sacrifice of Jesus which he, Jesus, intended making in his own time and place. Does this remove all guilt from Judas? It does not but can we not see that even in his act of betrayal the purpose of God in Christ, and no one else, was overruling? No man has the final word, only God has this, and we shall be wise not to spend time speculating on the fate of Judas but rather see how without knowing it he was actually in God's hands.

We are in deep water. Of course we are. We could say there has to be a villain in a play or there would be no play. So Judas filled the place someone had to fill. This could lead us into a learned discussion about the rival ideas of predestination and freewill leaving us little the wiser. Instead I wish to draw your attention to an aspect of the crucifixion which the part played by Judas highlights. The physical agonies of Jesus are beyond our imagining, so horrible were they, but there was another kind of suffering which we are able to imagine because we may have experienced it. This is to be let down by someone very close to us, someone whom we have trusted, above all someone whom we have loved. There are some verses in Psalm 41 about this kind of pain. 'All mine enemies whisper together against me: even against me do they imagine this evil . . . Yea, even mine own familiar friend, whom I trusted: who did eat of my bread, has laid wait for me.' Jesus knew this psalm and it must have pierced his soul when Judas approached him in the garden of Gethsemane in the company of men with swords and clubs come to arrest him and said 'Master!' and kissed him. This was the end. Jesus' heart must have broken then. Betrayed with a kiss! He would have to suffer all manner of physical torments in the hours immediately ahead but was there any suffering greater than that caused by that kiss of one he had made his friend? It is just possible that at this point in the crucifixion narrative we may be able to enter a little, I said 'a little', into what Christ suffered for us, if indeed it was for us. We shall not, most of us, know in experience anything like crucifixion, thank God, but what about being let down by someone who was dearly loved? Are there not women and men in increasing numbers today who know what this feels like and not only in broken marriages? We can be sure God will hear the cry of the broken-hearted for Christ's heart was broken in this way by Judas Iscariot. When we think of this the well-known words of Isaiah 53 strike home: 'Surely he hath borne our griefs, and carried our sorrows: yet we did esteem him stricken, smitten of God, and afflicted. But he was wounded for our transgressions, he was bruised for our iniquities: the chastisement of our peace was upon him; and with his stripes we are healed.'

4

THE LONELINESS OF LEADERSHIP

Behold, the hour cometh, yea, is now come, that ye shall be scattered, every man to his own, and shall leave me alone: and yet I am not alone, because the Father is with me.

JOHN 16.32

I would like you to think for a moment of a young man anxious, as we say, to 'get on' in life. Possessed of a quick brain, sound health, an ability to mix happily with people, he could be the head of a large firm, or possibly a Member of Parliament, then a Minister, then Cabinet rank; who knows what might follow? All very exciting, all very rewarding, but has he considered the cost? If you become a leader, if you climb to the top, you are bound to be lonely. The situation is comparable to a mountaineer. To be up on the roof of the world certainly brings a thrill, you feel good to have achieved it, but *you are alone*. This is the price to pay. So with the leader of any great organization. You reap benefits, but also the kicks, the complaints, the blame when anything goes wrong, and the jealousies and resentments. If you cannot fight alone, do not aspire to leadership.

Now Jesus was a leader. In the epistle to the Hebrews he is called the leader, the *archegos*, of our salvation. It meant being alone. Alone in temptation, alone in prayer, alone in conflicts, alone as a preacher and teacher; but never so alone as when he came to complete the work he came to do in the crucifixion. Even so the ultimate loneliness was not on the cross for crowds were there to gape, the depth of consummate loneliness was reached a few hours before in the garden of Gethsemane.

1 THE GARDEN CALLED GETHSEMANE

I want to tell you about that garden, and I do so as a relief from the terrifying agony which is the subject of this sermon. The account in the gospels of what happened there must be authentic for not even the most ardent admirer of a leader would invent a story like this. The garden lay on the slope of the Mount of Olives on the east of Jerusalem and derived its name from the oil press that once was there. Jesus loved this place. He was a frequent visitor using it as a retreat from the city streets, a place of prayer, perhaps also as a rendezvous for meeting people, and no doubt to call disciples to sit around while he taught them. I can't imagine anywhere on earth nearer heaven than that garden when Jesus was sitting there and talking. His sensitivity and language, his extraordinary personal presence, let alone the content of what he was saying must have transfixed the hearers. I have a garden and a corner in it with a bench and table where in the summer months I read and write. Please forgive the personal touch, I put it in so as to bring out the homeliness of this place for Jesus. Those of us who have passed most of our lives in big cities know what a garden, or even a park, can do for our personal wellbeing. This garden of Gethsemane did all that for Jesus and it turned out to be the last place in his life on earth to which he was free to go. It was there, however, that his soul was crucified as his body was a few hours later on Skull Hill not far away. Judas betrayed Jesus in this garden and that with a kiss.

I had it in mind not to include this unspeakably awful event in this series of sermons on the crucifixion on the grounds that I might be overweighting the series with too much descriptive material to the detriment of a proper emphasis on the meaning of the cross and passion for us today, but I have relented. I have relented because it is all too easy to see the crucifixion exclusively in terms of physical torture and this is a mistake. The physical torture was horrible enough but in the garden of Gethsemane Jesus suffered another kind of torture, the awfulness (I am using the word with care) we shall never be able wholly to plumb however much we know of heartbreak ourselves. Jesus was crucified by it, crucified therefore not only in body but in soul, and the crucifixion in soul took place in the garden he loved. It took place when he was alone. I am tempted to say the thought of Judas Iscariot become traitor crucified the soul of Jesus but truth to tell I am out of my depth; there is more in the agony in the garden than this, much more, so let me fall back now on description in so far as this is possible on the basis of the accounts we have in the gospels.

2 THE AGONY

The Last Supper in the upper room ended, the hymn sung, Jesus and the eleven disciples that remained after the defection of Judas descended to the streets outside. Dimly lit by the full Passover moon though they were, the group was not conspicuous for there was much coming and going in preparation for the festival the following day. Through the city wall they went and out east across the Kidron now babbling noisily in full flood, then up the slope of the Mount of Olives and into the garden of Gethsemane. On the way Jesus shocked the eleven disciples with the announcement that this would be the last time they would be together as a unit. The shepherd would be smitten and the sheep would be scattered. Peter protested his readiness to die in order to resist this, as did they all, but Jesus intimated that he would soon be completely alone.

Inside the garden gate he bid his disciples wait while he went forward to a spot further on, pointing to it possibly with his hand. Was it then that the utter loneliness of what was to befall him began to come in like a flood? He craved human companionship a little longer. He was human. He bade three disciples go with him, the three he had taken before on occasions of special solemnity like the raising of Jairus's daughter to life, and the Transfiguration scene, Peter, James and John, the men closest to him. Then even these were left while he moved still further into the garden in order to pray, though they could just see him and hear him. He was alone, utterly alone.

What these men saw and heard must have terrified them. They had never seen anything like it on the part of Jesus. Normally so strong, so unperturbed, so master of every and any circumstance, he was now completely crumpled up. He fell to the ground, flat on his face he fell, writhing in agony as if he had been hit. If this was praying to his heavenly Father it was unbelievable. There was shouting and crying, pleading and beseeching. The three disciples, able to see a little, scarcely recognized the face they knew so well now blood-smeared with the sweating intensity of what looked like a death struggle. Even the ground where he writhed in agony, it was said, was pitted with great drops of blood. Half hidden, they caught the words of his praying. 'Father, if it be possible, let this cup pass from me but not my will but thine be done.' For how long this agony continued the disciples did not know. Was it a whole hour during which time so exhausted were they they fell asleep? And Jesus longing then for human companionship in his utter loneliness walked over to them and rebuked Peter. 'Asleep, Simon? Were you not able to keep awake for one hour?' But they could not. He returned therefore to his praying alone and they to their sleeping together. But the end had to come and that swiftly. There was a scuffle at the garden gate. Torches, lanterns, swords and clubs were in evidence. And Judas leading the way into the garden he knew so well and behind him a crowd from the chief priests, scribes and elders come to arrest the man on whom for a great while they had longed to get their hands. A token resistance was made by at least one of the disciples but in a flash they took to their heels leaving their leader alone, his enemies pressing close around him.

3 THE LONELY CONFLICT

And now we ask what really was the agony in the garden of Gethsemane. Was it apprehension about the impending crucifixion? We can understand this. Who is there who does not fear physical pain? Jesus was a human being, even the most sensitive and finely tuned human being that has ever lived. Does it surprise us if the night before his crucifixion was one of horror? And that he was terrorized by it brings him closer to the level at which we live. He was not impervious to the thought of pain, nor are we.

But is this all? Is it really all? We shall never even begin to comprehend the real agony in the garden unless we keep in mind the Incarnation. 'In him was life', wrote St John in the magnificent prologue to his gospel, and 'the life was the light of men.' Jesus was the Word of God incarnate, the creative word. Death has no part in the Creator and therefore none in Jesus. It was alien to him. It belongs to the realm of darkness as he belongs to the realm of light. But he went there, was a stranger there and wholly out of place. The aloneness of Jesus thus became horrendous there.

Something else must be said. If all this was the lone battle Jesus, the incarnate Christ, fought for the reconciliation of sinful mankind to God would not the forces of spiritual evil gather themselves together to frustrate, and that finally, this lone attempt by this one man on earth to destroy all that for which they stood? It would be a devilish battle and it was, pitched in the very soul of Jesus. Backwards and forwards it raged, till he prayed 'O my Father, if this cup may not pass from me except I drink it, thy will be done'. Then he drank it to the dregs, the cup filled to the brim with the sins of the world. Symbolic words? Yes but with what other words can an agony unable to be couched in words be described? All this is beyond us. The garden of Gethsemane is where we cannot go. It is out of our reach.

4 BACK TO A BASIC SIMPLICITY

Is all this tension too great for us to sustain in a sermon? Let us therefore pick out one simple point to carry away. 'Not my will but thine be done' was Jesus' prayer. This must ever be in the forefront of our praying. We should never kneel simply to ask God to do what we want but to bring ourselves to do what he wants. Time and time again we feel our prayers have gone unanswered and we question the value of praying at all. Could it be however that sometimes they are unanswered so that we may be stripped of our inveterate self-concern? A few days ago I read of a young man who, angry with God, because of his apparently unanswered prayers betook himself to a spiritual guide, a man who had retreated from the world. 'Go and take that basket', he said, 'that dirty one over there, fill it with water, bring it here and fill this trough.' The young man did so. He was told to do it again. Then he protested. 'It is impossible to carry water in a basket, besides the basket is dirty.' 'I know', said the wise old man, 'but in attempting to do it you have cleaned the dirty basket, so your activity was worth it. Perhaps, young man, your unanswered prayers have cleansed you of your self-centredness. They have been worth it. Prayer is not getting God to do what you want but getting round to asking what he wants.' 'Thy will be done.' This is what Jesus prayed in the garden, quite alone.

5

THE GREAT CONFESSION

Again the high priest asked him, 'Are you the Christ, the Son of the Blessed?' And Jesus said, 'I am;...'

MARK 14.61–6 (RSV)

Almost every day when we open our newspapers we are confronted with some law case. It may concern forgery, drug offences, rape, burglary and, with sickening frequency, murder. The court proceedings are seldom brief, more often than not they are protracted, and frequently the accused has been held in custody for some weeks, even months, before the case actually opens. It was not like that for what must be reckoned the most significant trial in history—the trial and condemnation of Jesus of Nazareth. The whole thing was over—the arrest, the trial, verdict and the carrying out of the sentence completed in less than 24 hours. The hurry was intense. Why? This is what I must spell out in the crucifixion event.

1 POPULAR ANTICIPATION

Jesus was a divisive figure from the moment he began his ministry. This in itself is testimony to his stature. Who was he? No one bothers about an insignificant man but soon everyone was talking about Jesus of Nazareth. Only the very ignorant in Galilee and Judaea could be unaware of his existence. Crowds gathered to catch a glimpse of him, listen to his preaching, revel in his repartee with his opponents and marvel at his healing powers. No wonder those who knew the Scriptures recalled the words, 'Then shall the eyes of the blind be opened, the ears of the deaf be unstopped, then shall the lame man leap as an hart and the tongue of the dumb shall sing'. This was prophesied of the messianic age one day to dawn. Was it surprising then that when people encountered the ministry of Jesus they wondered whether the time had come, and he, Jesus was the promised Messiah?

But he never openly said he was, that was the trouble. So opinions were divided. The general public was divided. Not even religious people could make up their minds, indeed they were the most agitated of all about the identity of Jesus. And those in the seats of power in the land were afraid of civil disturbance. Moreover when any one of the great religious festivals took place in Jerusalem, especially the Passover, anxiety mounted to fever point. Everyone was asking, 'Will he come to the festival, do you think? Will this be the great moment of disclosure of the Messiah and the beginning of the messianic age? Will the massive power of the Romans be rolled back and we see something with which only the great exodus under Moses will compare?' The excited anticipation was widespread. And then six days before the great Passover festival for which the crowds flocked into Jerusalem from far and wide, Jesus rode like a king, albeit only on a little donkey, into the city itself, the crowds mad with delight and roaring 'Hosanna, blessed is he that cometh in the name of the Lord'. The rulers of the people were desperate. Something had to be done to discredit this man and get him out of the way. He could of course be held in custody for nine days, by which time the crowds who might rise up in support of him had gone home. But this was risky and how arrest him anyway? Then the unbelievable happened. A defector among the closest band of his followers made contact with the priests ready to disclose for a petty sum of money where they could lay hold of him. They could hardly believe their good fortune. How they must have rubbed their hands in glee!

2 THE ARREST OF JESUS

This is what happened. Judas, the traitor, it appears told the chief priests that Jesus could safely be arrested on the eve of the Passover when he would be observing the festival with his disciples. At the last moment he would inform them exactly where. He did so and the priests' officers arrived, but they were too late. The upper room indicated was empty. Jesus with his disciples had left and entered the nearby garden of Gethsemane where, as Judas knew, he often went to pray. He did pray there. It was an agonizing prayer. He prayed that if it were possible he might be spared the crucifixion but ended submissively 'Not my will but thine be done'. He had scarcely finished before a band of soldiers with swords and cudgels burst on the scene headed by Judas who hurried

21

forward to identify with a kiss whom the soldiers were to arrest. So Jesus was taken—bound and marched into the city to the house of Annas, the father-in-law of Caiaphas the high priest, where he was questioned closely. This gave time for the news to be relayed to the 71 members of the Great Sanhedrin (the Supreme Jewish Council) in their houses scattered across the city. We can imagine messengers hurrying breathlessly along the deserted streets knocking on doors and delivering the urgent and unexpected summons to a council. There was no time to lose. So Jesus found himself facing a formidable array of judges presided over by Caiaphas.

No one admired Caiaphas. He was the son-in-law of the hated Annas, once high priest himself (AD 7–14), who schemed to have his five sons elected to that high office, and later his son-in-law Caiaphas. All were more political than religious, aristocratic and wealthy. This was the man before whom Jesus stood bound as a prisoner. His one aim was to kill the prisoner not to try him but there had to be the semblance of a trial in order to have the weight of the Supreme Council behind whatever action he took. So a legal procedure was initiated. Witnesses were sought to charge Jesus with having said that he would destroy the Temple. Two at least were necessary and two were found; since however their testimony did not tally the case had to be dropped. So far the law was being scrupulously followed. Caiaphas was desperate. Jesus made no reply to any of the charges brought against him. Exasperated therefore he stood up and put the direct question to Jesus on which he knew everything depended. 'Are you the Messiah, the Son of the Blessed One?' The silence in the hall must have been deathly. To this Jesus did reply, he said 'I am; and you will see the Son of Man seated on the right hand of Power and coming with the clouds of heaven'. His use of the divine name 'I AM' was stunning. Caiaphas, enraged, tore his robes. 'Need we any further witnesses?' he cried out. 'You have heard the blasphemy. What is your opinion?' The assembled legal men were unanimous. Jesus was guilty. He should be put to death. Uproar followed. They spat on the prisoner and laid about him with their fists taunting him with the word 'Prophesy!' Caiaphas' men in particular set upon him with blows. All semblance of law and order vanished.

Still Caiaphas was not free of his difficulties. Court proceedings conducted at night carried no legal weight. So hastily in the morning a grand assembly was called. The elders of the nation were summoned, chief priests, doctors of the law, indeed all the leading people resident in the city in order to ratify the decision made during the night to put Jesus to death. The very size of the assembly would give the impression that the whole nation wished to be rid of the dangerous blasphemer. The numbers must have run well into three figures and the occasion uproarious for not everyone was in agreement. The great majority however rose up and brought Jesus to Pilate who alone had the authority for carrying out the death sentence. Somehow he must be persuaded that Jesus was politically dangerous. Everything depended on this. And so three charges were made before Pilate concerning the prisoner. He has subverted the nation, he is opposed to paying taxes to Caesar, and claims to be Messiah, a king.

Pilate no doubt looked the prisoner up and down and listened to the charges. The case was in his hands now, not Caiaphas's hands. Caiaphas waited. If Pilate gave sentence against Jesus it would mean crucifixion, and crucifixion meant complete discrediting in the eyes of all the Jewish people, for did not Deuteronomy 21.23 read 'for a hanged man is accursed by God'? Jesus would be publicly hanged on a cross, crucified, in Roman fashion.

3 THE IDENTITY OF THE CRUCIFIED JESUS

So Jesus was condemned to death because at the very last moment before the Supreme Council of the Jewish people of his time he confessed that he, the Son of man was the Messiah, that is the Christ. It was the first time that he had openly made this confession but it could scarcely have been made at a more significant time—Passover week—nor in a more significant place—the whole assembly of the Jewish people in Jerusalem. If up to this last moment Jesus had been, as it were, a secret Messiah he was so no longer. He was the self-confessed Messiah declared with the maximum publicity.

But was he guilty? Is he? Is he the Messiah, the Christ or must he be counted a blasphemer? Maybe we would like the question to go away. We would like to be left with some such simple confession that Jesus was a good man, a caring man, a brilliant teacher. But was he crucified because of his goodness? And if he was, have not many relatively good people been tortured to death in this century? On this view what the crucifixion does is paint in lurid colours a picture of man's inhumanity to man. The cross then stands as a stark commentary on the state of our world. So why set it up in our churches, *on* our churches or anything to be marked as Christian? There is no hope in it, no uplift, certainly no Gospel, only a reminder of what we already know. There is nothing new.

It may be that in listening to me you have doubted if it really is necessary to recount in such detail the story of the arrest, trial and crucifixion of Jesus. It all happened so long ago and much 'water has passed under the bridge' since then. But, you see, everything about the Christian faith actually turns on the identity of him who was crucified. We believe, the Church has consistently believed that he was the Christ. We speak of *Christ* crucified. But is this merely a pious hope, an idea, something thought up to give the Church significance? Did anyone outside the ranks of the disciples of Jesus ever hear him make the claim himself, anyone with no vested interest? The answer is, yes, one man, Caiaphas supported by a whole assembly of legal men gathered together in Jerusalem. They heard his answer 'I am' to the question 'Are you the Christ, the Son of the Blessed?' and they had him crucified for it. This is why the Scripture which I have retold in this sermon is of overwhelming importance. It tells us that the man on the cross is not only suffering in company with thousands upon thousands of other men and women and that nobly but that he was God incarnate. So there is nothing like this crucifixion in all the world nor ever has been. It stands by itself ready to cast its light even upon our darkest hours. We must not pass it by. We must try to hear not only what it says, but what it offers. Everything of eternal worth is centred there.

> In the Cross of Christ I glory,
> Towering o'er the wrecks of time;
> All the light of sacred story
> Gathers round its head sublime.

6

PONTIUS PILATE AND HIS WIFE

'Have nothing to do with that innocent man; I was much troubled on his account in my dreams last night.'

MATTHEW 27.19 (NEB)

This is Good Friday and I have to talk to you about Pontius Pilate. It is not possible to ignore Pontius Pilate when considering the crucifixion because he ordered it. We are made conscious of him every time we repeat the Creed—'suffered under Pontius Pilate, was crucified, dead, and buried'. All four gospels give an account of him in the trial scenes, and the fourth gospel, St John's, appointed to be read on Good Friday, brings him to our notice more vividly than the others. Who was he? He was the Governor, technically Procurator, of Judaea and must have been at least 27 to hold that position. He was of course a Roman appointed to his office by the Emperor Tiberius, and a military man. Pilate, or Pilatus, means he once carried a *pilum*, or javelin, in the army. A tough man, but in other ways a weak man. I am always sorry for Pilate, and I think Jesus was, but I will come to that later.

He was educated of course, belonging to upper middle-class Roman society and civilized according to those standards. He lived in considerable comfort both in his palace down by the Mediterranean Sea and in the Governor's residence when he came to Jerusalem on business. He was married and his wife was devoted to his welfare or she would never have come to live in (to her) boring Jerusalem with its religious fanaticism, exchanging for it the society of sophisticated Rome. What is more she actually stayed with him during the politically explosive season of the Jewish Passover. In short this woman cared for Pilate her husband. She saw something in him under that stiff military exterior; but then love often does when no one else sees anything very much. She appears on a page of the New Testament because she had a dream, a dream about Jesus; and whenever dreams are mentioned in the Bible they refer to God speaking to people. So here was God speaking to this pagan society woman.

25

We cannot be blamed for wondering how this came about; but no one could of course even stir in the province of Judaea without information about it being reported to the Governor's office. Pilate would certainly know about Jesus, and we may be certain his wife knew. They may have discussed him in private. Was he dangerous or a harmless religious type? Jewry abounded with these. Was he a political danger, or simply a spiritual teacher? Had she actually seen him in Jerusalem? More than likely she had heard of that (to her) comic little procession—Jesus seated on a little donkey as if he were some kind of king. Jesus puzzled her. She had heard of his healings of sick people and his kindness to women. Perhaps she had disguised herself and mingled in the crowds to watch him.

1 THE DREAM

And now early on the Friday morning this very man, this Jesus, was in her husband's power, delivered to him by a coterie of jealous priests. On a trumped-up charge he was up for trial. She awoke from her sleep to realize that even now at this early hour Pilate was sitting on his judgement seat bound to pass sentence on this man who had captured her attention, even more, her sympathy. And so, greatly daring, she dispatched a messenger into the very courtroom where her husband was already conducting the trial with the urgent message 'Have nothing to do with this innocent man; I was much troubled on his account in my dreams last night'.

Note that Pilate had no dream. God did not speak to him before he moved from his bedchamber to sit on the judgement seat and the strange, beaten, yet commanding figure was stationed before him, his hands tied. They looked each other in the eyes—Pilate and Jesus of Nazareth, Jesus of Nazareth and Pilate, both possibly about the same age. And then the knock on the door and the urgent message, 'Have nothing to do with that innocent man; I was much troubled on his account in my dreams last night'.

2 WOMAN'S INTUITION

Observe how God did not speak to the man who had power, he spoke to the woman who had no power. What she had was sensitivity, intuition as women have. She understood Jesus in a way her man, Pilate, never did, perhaps never could. Do not miss the point. Power does not necessarily provide insight. It may even impede insight. Perhaps nowadays those women who are clamouring for power and the seats of power need to remember this. And men would do well to listen to women. They can often sense the spiritual dimension to life and what are the real springs of action in an individual to which men, some men, are almost blind. Power does not sharpen the qualities of the soul. It is more likely to dull them. And when God speaks women may hear, where men, even intellectuals, hear nothing at all. This little side-show scene on Good Friday about the Lady Claudia Procula, Pilate's wife, if such was her name, reminds us to take woman's intuition seriously. Terrible mistakes are sometimes avoided that way. Perhaps Pilate would not have condemned Jesus to crucifixion and his name be ever after in the Creed.

And now I wonder, I do not know but I wonder, when Pilate's wife had delivered her message did she creep over to the courtroom door and listen outside? Did she overhear her husband say, in that clipped military Latin voice of his, 'I find no fault in this man'. Did she breath a sigh of relief? But what was that sound of water being poured into a basin? Was Pilate washing his hands? But why? In heaven's name why? And then the horrible verdict and Pilate barking out 'Take him and crucify him yourselves. I find no fault in him.'

Poor Lady Claudia Procula. Did she wring her hands? Did she creep back to bed? Did she lie there listening to the blood-curdling cries of the crowds outside, 'Crucify him'? Did she in imagination see that lonely figure treading the pathway to the crucifixion site? She had told Pilate her husband what she had already suffered in a dream because of the man he held in his power as he sat on the judgement seat, but the bad dream was nothing in comparison with what she suffered now wide awake as she thought of Jesus being hoisted up on that horrible cross just outside the city wall and her own residence.

The wife of Pilate was a pagan woman but she suffered for Christ's sake. She suffered as she lay on her bed that Good Friday morning. And this is the question I ask myself, did not her tears that day put her into the salvation which Christ came into the world to bring, although she did not know one word of Christian doctrine? When I think of this lady in the Governor's residence it comes home to me once again how wide open is the gate for the reception of eternal life which can be ours. 'Whosoever will may come.' 'He/she who comes to me I will in no wise cast out.' Do not forget Pilate's wife. She has her place in God's eternal kingdom, of this I am absolutely sure. She suffered for him and no one who suffers for him can possibly be lost.

3 PILATE THE GOVERNOR

And now Pilate the Governor, her husband. There is nothing more strange in the whole history of the world than the interview that took place on Good Friday morning between this Roman and Jesus of Nazareth. There were in fact two interviews. First Pilate examined him after he had come straight from the High Priest's Court. The second was after Pilate had flogged him and exhibited him to the crowds wearing that ridiculous crown of thorns and a purple cloak, the whole cruel farce designed to humiliate the Jews whom Pilate despised. 'This is the sort of crumpled king you ought to have!' Jesus stood there. '*Ecce homo*' Pilate barked out. 'Behold the man.' But Pilate's curiosity was aroused. Jesus did not seem to be in the least afraid of him. 'Don't you know that I have power to release you and power to crucify you?'

Why was not Jesus afraid of Pilate? I think I can tell you—because he loved him. Do you not remember what St John, the author of the gospel where this interview is recorded, wrote in his epistle? 'There is no fear in love; but perfect love casteth out fear.' And we may be sure that Jesus, who could read people, saw how weak Pilate really was for all the panoply of his power. Pilate wanted to release Jesus. Had he not received his wife's message and been disturbed by it? But he crucified Jesus because if he did not he would be accused of incompetence to govern a turbulent province like Judaea and that would spell the end of his career. So he caved in. I said earlier on that I feel sorry for Pilate. I am sure Jesus felt far more than sorrow, he actually loved him, which was why he was not in the least afraid of him even though he could barely stand after the lashes of those torturous whips fiercely laid on him by the brutal soldiers.

There is an ancient Jewish story which runs as follows, and if I have told it before, I apologize, but in any case it is worth repeating. An old Rabbi once asked his pupils what was the precise hour when night ended and day began. The pupils thought hard. 'Is it', one of them asked, 'when you can tell the difference between a sheep and a dog? Or a date palm from a fig tree?' The Rabbi shook his head. 'What is it then?' demanded the impatient pupils. The Rabbi answered 'It is when you can look into the face of anyone and see there your sister or your brother. Until then it is still night for you.'

Jesus looked into the face of Pontius Pilate and was not afraid of him. 'There is no fear in love; but perfect love casteth out fear.'

And so the summary of the gospel as we have it in John 3.16: 'God so loved the world, that he gave his only begotten Son, that whosoever . . .' Whosoever? You mean the Lady Claudia Procula? The Roman centurion standing on guard by the cross? That nameless bandit crucified on Good Friday alongside Jesus? Simon all the way from Cyrene? And Joseph of Arimathea, sufficiently well-to-do to have his own tomb near Jerusalem cut out of the rock ready for him when he died?—high and low, rich and poor, one with another? Yes all of these and many more. Whosoever allows his or her heart to be warmed towards Jesus, 'whosoever believeth in him, shall not perish but have eternal life'. I have invited you today to catch a glimpse of the extraordinary breadth of the love of God and of the Christian Gospel by looking at it through the window of the Lady Claudia Procula, wife of Pontius Pilate who crucified Jesus.

7

NOTHING TO SAY

Then he questioned him in many words; but he answered him nothing.

LUKE 23.9

If you read this verse aloud you should make a significant pause before the last word. 'Then he questioned him in many words; but he answered him . . . nothing.' The RSV is weak in comparison, 'but he made no answer', and fails to catch the force of the Greek. Here are two men facing each other, the one talking, talking, talking; the other offering . . . nothing. Who are they? The talkative one is Herod the tetrarch of Galilee, the other is Jesus of Nazareth. The place is Herod's palace in Jerusalem and the time a few hours before the Crucifixion. This is why I suggest we think about it.

1 HEROD ANTIPAS

First Herod, rigged up as a king and called 'King Herod', but in fact he was only a puppet king; the final authority lay with the Roman Governor appointed by the Emperor Tiberius. But Rome with its genius for governing diverse national groups in its vast empire let them call their governors 'Kings' in order to keep their allegiance. Such was Herod Antipas, governor of Galilee from 4 BC to AD 39, all the years of Jesus' life.

What sort of man was this Herod? Crudely expressed, he was 'no good'. He wasn't a patch on his father Herod the Great who, in spite of his cruelty and cunning, had a measure of greatness in him, hence his title. Antipas on the contrary was a little man, puffed up, licentious and weak, manipulated by his wife Herodias the ex-wife of his brother Herod Philip, a nasty woman not above degrading her own daughter Salome in order to squeeze out of her new husband what she wanted. You can read about it in Mark, chapter 6, only the half isn't told. Herod Antipas, weak with women, was trapped by Herodias into having John the Baptist, the forerunner of Jesus in the ministry, murdered. Not that he wanted this; he was, truth to tell, fascinated by John, not least, strange as it may sound, on account of his preaching of divine judgement. So when, horrified, he stared at the gruesome severed head brought up from the dungeon he was for ever after haunted by what he had done. And when not long after he was told about Jesus, teaching, healing and drawing in the crowds in the very region of Galilee where he had caused John the Baptist to be incarcerated he suffered bad dreams. 'This is John', he said, 'whom I beheaded, risen from the dead.' This was the man Jesus faced only a matter of hours before his crucifixion and questioned in many words 'but he answered him . . . nothing'.

2 THE PHARISEES' TRAP

There is one other incident we must consider before we come to the interview when Herod 'questioned Jesus in many words; but he answered him . . . nothing'. It is recorded in Luke, chapter 13. A number of Pharisees approached Jesus with the warning 'You should leave this place and go on your way; Herod is out to kill you'. Was he? So might we now be repeating in our churches Sunday by Sunday not 'suffered under Pontius Pilate, was crucified, dead, and buried' but 'suffered under *Herod Antipas*, was murdered, dead and buried'? But it didn't happen. Herod did indeed hate the reports that filtered through to him of the powerful ministry of Jesus in his territory but he had no wish to be responsible for another murder. He would rather someone else had blood on their hands for liquidating Jesus. The Pharisees knew this. They knew their Herod. What is more they themselves wanted Jesus engineered south into Judaea where they would have a better chance of getting a hold on him. So they slyly said to Jesus, 'You should leave this place, Herod is seeking to kill you'. All very subtle. All very cunning, but Jesus was not taken in: he replied, 'Go and tell that fox (Herod Antipas), "Behold, I cast out demons and perform cures today and tomorrow, and the third day I finish my course. Nevertheless I must go on my way today and tomorrow and the day following; for it cannot be that a prophet should perish away from Jerusalem." ' Did the Pharisees understand what he meant? Did Jesus expect them to understand? Did they go and report his words to Herod, that fox?—a fierce and cunning animal. It is most unlikely.

31

3 THE INTERVIEW

And now the interview when Herod 'questioned Jesus in many words; but he answered him . . . nothing'. The occasion was unexpected and unplanned. Herod found Jesus, whom he had long wished to see, standing before him. He was there because Pilate was desperate to get Jesus off his hands. He reckoned that there was no case for Jesus to answer but the chief priests were bent on pressing a case. Pilate thought he saw a way out of his impasse. Hearing that Jesus was a Galilean and therefore could be said to come under Herod's jurisdiction he sent him to Herod who was in Jerusalem at that time. We may guess Pilate breathed again. And Herod for his part was jubilant. Here was Pilate recognizing his authority at last instead of continuing to ignore him. And here too was the chance for which he had been longing, namely actually to see this Jesus of whom he had heard so much. Perhaps he would perform a miracle. What fun! And for the court too! But the occasion fell flat. There was no miracle. Jesus did not even speak, not even when the chief priests and lawyers appeared pressing their case against him. Herod felt insulted. He would 'get his own back' on Jesus for that woodenness in his presence. Assisted by his troops he dressed Jesus up in a gorgeous robe to express his contempt and ridicule. Then he returned Pilate's reject back to himself. He pictured Pilate's face when the door was opened and in was marched Jesus, this time all dressed up. All this made Herod's day. He was that sort of man.

4 TWO REASONS FOR CHRIST'S SILENCE

And now we return to the text, Luke 23.9: 'Then he questioned him in many words; but he answered . . . nothing'. Are we to understand from this that there are occasions when Christ, when God has nothing to say to us, pile on as many words, as many questions as we like? Are we to understand that the crucifixion may have nothing to say to us, no word from God, no word of God? I am afraid that this is what this scripture is crying aloud to tell us. There are at least, I think two reasons and the first is when the crucifixion is not considered beyond the level of politics, the politics of the time. I admit that this can be, indeed is, a subject of absorbing interest. At one level the crucifixion was threaded through with politics. Caiaphas, the High Priest, was motivated by the political

32

necessity, as he read the situation, of speedily bringing about the death of Jesus lest the whole nation be torn apart by the upsurge of popular rival factions for and against Jesus. And where did the Roman authority fit into all this? And what were the intrigues in progress between the opposing parties? And have even the accounts of the trials and crucifixion of Jesus in the New Testament been written up, even perhaps unconsciously, with a political bias? There is material here for almost endless discussion, if not academic research. And if we fall for this approach to the crucifixion and never rise beyond it, then we shall, I fear, hear no word from God, no word of God, in this event. We may question in many words but God will answer . . . nothing.

Secondly we shall encounter nothing but silence at the crucifixion if like Herod Antipas we cannot or will not throw off our shallowness and sheer superficiality when we are confronted with it. Some of you may remember how, not so very long ago, a drawing was published of a naked Christ on the cross with outsize genitals. What could a mind, artist's or not, so soaked in and warped by sex hear of God's word in the crucifixion? Surely nothing. Jesus had nothing to say to Herod when stood before him bound as a captive. Did Jesus at that moment think of his own words as recorded in the Sermon on the Mount (Matthew 7.6): 'Give not that which is holy unto the dogs, neither cast ye your pearls before swine, lest they trample them under their feet, and turn again and rend you'? Pigs do not know the worth of pearls, they will not differentiate between them and the engulfing mud. Words can be pearls, words of wisdom. The words of Christ were that and much more, but the Herods of this world will neither recognize them nor appreciate them, they will trample them under their feet. This is why Jesus had nothing to say to Herod a few hours before his crucifixion.

There is a terrible verse in Hosea, chapter 4 in the Old Testament which reads 'Ephraim is joined to idols: let him alone'. There are times, places and occasions when any kind of preaching or testimony is out of place. Then the servants of God had better keep their mouths tightly shut. Perhaps we in our commendable enthusiasm for the Decade of Evangelism ought to bear this in mind. A word in season is the only word that ought to be spoken. Evangelists, of all people, ought to be sensitive to seasons, but so ought ordinary Church people who are not ashamed or afraid to confess their faith.

All the scenes pertaining to the crucifixion are sad in varying degrees. Insensitive would be the reader of the account of them in the four gospels who was in no way moved. It is sad to think of Herod Antipas so deaf to anything fine and spiritual by the time Christ appeared before him that speaking to him would be worse than useless. Poor Herod that he had sunk so low! I am sure Christ pitied him. You will notice that he did not upbraid Herod, nor speak to him of a coming day of judgement, he left him alone. This is terrible but sometimes it has to be. Perhaps this is how we ought to understand hell, to be left alone by God. I don't know. All I feel I can do in the presence of this scripture about Herod is to leave the story where it is and not write it off as having nothing to say to me, not least about the crucifixion.

8

FOUR SOLDIERS

Then they sat down and kept watch over him there.
MATTHEW 27.36 (RSV)

I am tempted to omit this sermon altogether but it would seem illogical
to preach a course of sermons on the crucifixion and leave out the event
itself. I am tempted because it would be possible in preaching it to
present a lurid description of what happened at Golgotha, that ghastly
place of execution, as some writers and painters have done, but this
would be contrary to the New Testament presentation. All four gospels
do indeed describe the crucifixion. They do not simply record it, but
what they have given us is restrained, there is nothing like a horror story.
I shall observe this reticence when I present it from the point of view of
the four Roman soldiers who actually carried out the crucifixion and
who, when they had finished what to them was a job, sat down and 'kept
watch over him there'.

1 THE SOLDIERS' WORK

They had begun their work in the Praetorium at Pilate's residence in
Jerusalem where the whole battalion of his soldiers had been assembled.
Here they lampooned Jesus, decking him out in a scarlet robe and crushing a handful of prickly twigs on his head crudely twisted to look like a
crown. A reed thrust into his hand completed the ludicrous semblance to
royalty, sufficient to encourage mock obeisance before him with the
acclaim 'Hail, King of the Jews'.

Then they stripped off the comic clothes, replacing them with his
own. He was marched along the crowded street to the place of execution
outside the city. The custom was to load the victim with the transom on
which the arms and hands were to be stretched and to prod him along the
way with goads and scourges. In front of him was carried a wooden

35

board, if he could not carry it himself, on which was inscribed the crime for which he was to be crucified. Everything was designed to humiliate the victim, reducing him to the level of a beast of burden being driven to the slaughterhouse.

On arrival at the awful site, an ugly skull-shaped hill sufficiently high to provide the avid spectators with a view, the four soldiers stripped Jesus of his clothes, which became their perks. They tossed for the best pieces. Jesus was offered a drink of drugged wine from a supply regularly provided by a guild of women in Jerusalem to dull the pain of the victims, but Jesus refused it. Then having attached the cross-piece, the transom, to the upright stake they nailed his hands to it. The feet were often tied, not nailed, and this may have been the case with Jesus (see John 20.25, 27). It was not an act of mercy, it actually prolonged the agony. The soldiers then fixed the board to the top of the upright stake, displaying the words 'Jesus the King of the Jews'. The cross with its victim, now assembled, was then hauled into the upright position and made firm in a hole. It was no great height, only sufficient for the feet to clear the ground. Two brigands were also crucified, one on each side of Jesus.

The four soldiers had worked hard completing these three crucifixions. When they had finished they sat down and refreshed themselves from a jar of *posca*, the vinegar which was allowed soldiers on duty. Seeing Jesus as a pretender both to Jewish and imperial power, they raised their cups in mock homage to him and drank His Majesty's health. The chief priests, the scribes and the elders of the Jewish people crowded round, joining in the ribald commentary. Then the soldiers sat down and 'kept watch over him there', guarding against any possibility of a rescue attempt. The centurion, or captain, in charge of the whole operation stood facing the crucified noting all that was taking place.

2 THE HUMILIATION

Words fail as instruments to portray the agonies of the crucified, and we must not omit the two brigands impaled alongside Jesus who suffered the same, if not worse, for they were 'finished off' with a heavy mallet as they hung dying. Jesus was spared this horror. And it is to be wondered if victims of the Nazi terror have not suffered equally. In the obituary notice for Klaus Barbie, the so-called 'butcher of Lyon' who died in

September 1991 aged 77, we were informed how 'Mme Lise Lesèrre had been continually tortured by him for nineteen days. He had her hung from the ceiling by her wrists with spiked handcuffs until she fainted, tied her to a steel table, beaten with a bull whip, ripped her back open by lashing it with a spiked copper ball on the end of a chain, and repeatedly submitted her to bath torture which meant drowning just short of the point of death and then revived with blows. The list of such tortures', continued the obituary notice, 'could be indefinitely extended.' These crimes were committed secretly in dungeons and in specially designed chambers of horror. Crucifixion, on the contrary, and this includes that of Jesus, was carried out in public, everything calculated to humiliate. The body was stripped naked and spread-eagled out for the benefit of the public gaze, its physical functions, blood and sweat creating a nauseating stench. This was dying with indignity with a vengeance. Even a wild animal creeps into a hole when its end is near. This was not allowed for Jesus, he was exposed for as many as possible to enjoy his agony. There was no covering.

Can we say that the humiliation of crucifixion was even worse than the tortures? It was certainly designed to compound them. And the more elevated by nature, culture and spiritual awareness the victim, so much worse the degradation, for the greater the height, the greater the depth involved. How can we begin to grasp the humiliation of Jesus at Golgotha? The imagination reels. It was this depth of humiliation which dominated the mind of St Paul and impelled him to quote from the hymn (if it was a hymn): 'For the divine nature was his from the first; yet he did not think to snatch at equality with God, but made himself nothing, assuming the nature of a slave. Bearing the human likeness, revealed in human shape, he humbled himself, and in obedience accepted even death—death on a cross' (Philippians 2.6–8 NEB). Death on a cross! What death could be worse, what more humiliating?

Presumably it was left to the four soldiers to clear up after the crucifixion. There was a strange note of decency operating at Golgotha. According to Jewish religious scruples bodies were not to remain on the crosses during the Sabbath. A Sabbath followed Good Friday. The bodies therefore had to be taken down, odd as it must have seemed to the four Roman soldiers. For them it was customary to leave the bodies where they hung for wild animals to tear out the intestines and for birds to pick the bones. A crucifixion site after a crucifixion was ghastly. Foot passers-by chose to find another way. This did not happen after the crucifixion of Jesus. The soldiers disposed of the bodies of the two brigands, probably on the city's refuse dump where the scavenger dogs would find them. In the case of Jesus, to the soldiers' astonishment, no doubt, a well-to-do Jew, probably with servants, turned up reverently to take down his broken body and carefully to prepare it for decent, indeed honourable burial. Then the soldiers saw to the dismantling of the crosses and their removal. They had finished their job. They had cleaned up the site. They returned to their barracks and showed off their perks, the clothes of Jesus.

3 THE HISTORICAL FOUNDATION OF THE CHRISTIAN FAITH

I return to my text—Matthew 27.36: 'Then they sat down and kept watch over him there'. No one came closer to the crucifixion of Jesus than those four Roman soldiers. They not only saw him, they touched him, they handled him. The (to us) sacred body was delivered into their hands. They were the last people to touch that body. But we touch it. That is to say we touch his sacramental body. 'This is my body' said Jesus to his disciples in the upper room the night before he was crucified as he handed them bread which he had blessed *and broken*. This is what is repeated for us in every service of Holy Communion as we follow his command in remembrance of him. There is handed to us his sacramental broken body. This is what we receive. Unlike the four soldiers (poor men) we receive in faith and in so doing know that we enter into what the incarnate Christ did for us there.

> Here, O my Lord, I see thee face to face;
> Here faith would touch and handle things unseen;
> Here grasp with firmer hand the eternal grace,
> And all my weariness upon thee lean.
>
> (H. Bonar)

In repeating this Eucharistic hymn I have strayed from the plain historical event of the crucifixion which it has been my aim to highlight but I have done so in order to say that without some such spiritual interpretation we shall see little more in the event than did the four soldiers. We shall therefore in due course return to this aspect but I have not begun there. I have begun with the story of the crucifixion for it is there that the New Testament begins, and if we diminish this we undermine the Christian faith.

Hard questions, I know, may be asked of the story as we have it. For example, have the accounts in the four gospels been accommodated to the pattern of words in certain parts of the Old Testament? Has the early Church's experience of martyrdom caused the gospel accounts of the crucifixion to be presented as martyrology? How was it possible for the seven words from the Cross (as commonly called) to be heard and reported? There may not be easy answers to such questions but I have raised them lest you should think that we have been carried along by sentiment in the face of a heart-rending story. No, we have not rubbed out our critical faculty. When however all has been examined, discussed and argued over in the light of scholarship the cross still stands in history. *Jesus was crucified*, and if we believe him to be the incarnate Son of God, which is the Christian confession, nothing can be the same again in our understanding of God, the world, life and death. Everything is transformed. There cannot be Christianity without this crucifixion. It stands at the centre, for some as an offence, for others the ever-shining light of life, a brightly shining golden cross studded with jewels.

9

THE COMPLETION OF CHRIST'S WORK

I glorified thee on earth, having accomplished the work which thou gavest me to do.

JOHN 17.4 (RSV)

Almost everything about Jesus Christ is different. He was a human being as we are human beings but he was different. He was born of a mother as we are born of mothers but he was different. He died as we die but his death was different. I do not mean that it was different because he died on a cross and the number of people whose death is by crucifixion is infinitesimal in comparison with the totality of mankind, I mean his death was the climax of his ministry, not the point at which it died down. We are to picture the crucifixion of Jesus not as the fading-out point of his life's purpose, nor even as the point when his powers, while still effective, were cut short so that we want to cry 'How sad!' No, what we have to visualize is something more like a cross-country runner having traversed all manner of hazards and obstacles finally breasting the tape with sufficient breath in spite of exhaustion to call out 'I have done it, I have done it'. So my text, the words of Jesus himself: 'I glorified thee on the earth, having accomplished the work which thou gavest me to do'.

1 THE CRY OF SATISFACTION

Let me place the verse in its context, in the upper room the night before his crucifixion. I make no apology for going back there. No one can be a communicant Christian and lose sight of the upper room where the Lord was betrayed. After Judas, the traitor, had received the dipped bread handed to him by Jesus, he rose up, left the table and passed through the door out into the night to tell the chief priests where they could make an arrest without the risk of an uproar in the city. Jesus, consistently calm, was now deeply troubled, and when he watched that door close behind Judas, and perhaps heard his steps down the stairs outside, he knew the end of his incarnate life was at hand. Recovering his tranquillity however he spoke in depth to the eleven disciples intently listening. When he had finished his discourse he raised his eyes to heaven—one of the eleven who was there recalled every detail—and prayed, 'Father, the hour has come, glorify thy Son that the Son may glorify thee . . . I glorified thee on earth, having accomplished the work thou gavest me to do'. The prayer ended, altogether they sang the Passover hymn—what would we not give to hear them singing?—after which they trooped out to the Mount of Olives where Jesus was arrested, bound and marched back into the city for his trial—condemnation and execution.

And now we move on to the last moments of the crucifixion itself. The end was near. Not one word had Jesus uttered concerning his physical sufferings, but there came this, sufficiently audible for a response to be made, 'I thirst'. A jar full of sour wine stood nearby, so someone soaked a sponge with the wine, put it on the point of a javelin and held it to his lips. This enabled him to cry out one word with a voice so loud that it startled the centurion in charge of the crucifixion, the word in the Greek was the same word he had used in his final prayer of dedication in the upper room, *tetelestai*, 'It is accomplished'. And then, doubtless, almost a whispered prayer: 'Father, into thy hands I commend my spirit'. So, as the first words from the cross began with Father, 'Father forgive them; for they know not what they do', so did the last words. He had accomplished the work which the Father had given him to do. With his dying breath he shouted it out marking his triumph. He had done it, self-sacrifice to the uttermost, he had no more to give, he had given his all, nothing was held back, there was not even a cry of resentment at the torture.

Before we consider the precise nature of the work Jesus was conscious of having completed in the crucifixion let me draw your attention to one other passage of Scripture. It is in the letter to the Hebrews, chapter 12, verse 4. Who precisely were the recipients of this letter, and who wrote it, we cannot be sure, but this much is clear, it was written to exhort the recipients to put a braver face than they were doing up against their undoubtedly harsh opponents to the faith. 'You have not yet resisted to the point of shedding your blood' he wrote. But this was the advice how to proceed (verse 2): 'looking to Jesus the pioneer and perfecter of our faith, who for the joy that was set before him endured the cross, despising the shame, and is seated at the right hand of the throne of God'. Is this a picture of a fading out ministry? Is it not rather a picture of a supremely brave contestant in a terrible struggle who nevertheless wins and is acclaimed for his success? So much so that we are tempted to be satisfied with classing Jesus as a hero, which description however would be wholly inadequate. But let this picture of Jesus, glad to have accomplished his work as he did, remain with us. Not least it will help to counteract morbid approaches to the cross and passion of Christ which are wholly inappropriate to true Christian faith.

2 THE PERFECT SACRIFICE

We must now move on and face the consequence of seeing the crucifixion as the crowning point of the life and ministry of Jesus. This consequence is the recognition that until he breathed his last on the cross—'Father, into thy hands I commend my spirit'—he had definitely *not* completed what he had dedicated himself from the outset to do, namely, to offer the perfect sacrifice. It is true all his life was sacrificial. The Incarnation, taking our human nature upon himself was sacrificial. By doing this he humbled himself. And in that lowliness he was consistently obedient in reaching out to people in whatever depths they were or had fallen. This was evident from the outset of his ministry when at his baptism he joined the queue waiting to be baptized by John in the river Jordan, standing in with the motley crowd; some sincere, some pensive, many empty-headed, foolish and shallow; dirty people, smelly, broken down and shuffling; some idiots, no doubt led by a relative. Did they understand what they were doing? Repentance can be confusing. Jesus who knew no sin stood in with them. And he also faced the subtle and sometimes barefaced hostility of the religious intellectuals. And he sat down to eat and drink with the tricksters and scoundrels. What was more he endured the sheer woodenness of his own disciples which apparently at times all but drove him to despair. Let me repeat, all the life and ministry of Jesus was a sacrifice, but still until the crucifixion he had not completed his sacrifice.

There are those who try to tell us that the Sermon on the Mount is the apex of his ministry. It is what Jesus taught that gives him his significance—his incomparable parables, his unforgettable sayings both linguistically and in content, and his healings. To those who take this view to assert that his life and ministry was incomplete without the crucifixion is nonsense. But let me put it to you, even if it be conceded that the purpose of his life was to give the world an example of perfect obedience, and I, for my part, do not think the word 'example' anything like adequate, still it must be conceded that the example was lacking *until* he had made what today we would call 'the supreme sacrifice', until he had given up even life itself when he need not have done.

The crucifixion then is the place of the perfect sacrifice. It is the place of the perfection of love both to God and man. As he himself said in the upper room the night before his death, 'Greater love has no man than this that a man lay down his life for his friends' (John 15.13).

And so when Jesus followed not long after Judas out through the door of the upper room—Judas gone on ahead to betray his Master for money, Jesus going to his arrest, trial and crucifixion—he was actually placing the coping stone on all the incarnate life he had lived up to this point. Without the crucifixion it would stand as an incomplete building. Now therefore, when we stop and look at the cross we must say, 'there is *the perfect sacrifice*, the sacrifice without blot or stain, the sacrifice of the perfect, the perfect completed by sacrifice'. There is no distortion then in the story of Jesus as presented by all four gospels when they lead as they do, up to the crucifixion. This really was the climax of what Christ came to do.

3 OUR REPRESENTATIVE

I have mildly quarrelled with the word 'example'. I have done so because to present Jesus as primarily an example to us is devastating. If to be like Christ is to be the aim of my life I give up the struggle in despair. Love my enemies? Never hit back when I am insulted? No despising of the incompetent, the ham-fisted and foolish? No complaining about privation or pain? Always ready with 'a word in season'? What a hope! Impossible! If Christ is simply my copybook then count me out.

I am speaking personally, so let me go on. I see Christ differently. I see him as my representative. No, not as my substitute, not that I may now sit back in the pavilion, so to speak, while the struggle is waged for me. I still have to tackle life with fortitude but Christ as my representative makes up for my many imperfections, failures and sins. And he is not remote from me, he is not completely other than I am, he is not out on an altogether different plane; in the Incarnation he took *our nature* upon him and *in that nature* completed the perfect sacrifice I could never even begin to manage.

Yes, I am beginning to touch on deep issues concerning the crucifixion and how Christ could possibly represent us. To these we shall need to address ourselves in another sermon, accepting some interpretations and rejecting others, though recognizing that they may nevertheless have helped some to faith. For the moment let us be content to stand over against the crucifixion in a mood of thoughtful gratitude for what Christ accomplished there for us. 'Thanks be to God for his unspeakable gift.'

10

THE LABEL ON THE CROSS

And Pilate wrote a title also and put it on the cross.
JOHN 19.19 (RV)

We have a passion for labels in the modern world. We can't resist labelling people. Nowadays everyone has a tag attached—upper class, working class, democrat, manual worker, graduate, High Church, Charismatic. I could go on, so could you. And almost everything about a person is judged in the first place by the label, just like a product on the shelf in a supermarket.

1 PILATE'S LABEL

I remind you that Jesus had a label attached. Pilate wrote it out, or more likely he stood over someone who was told exactly what words to write. So it was Pilate's label for Jesus, or 'title' as St John calls it in his gospel, and he was, after all, an eyewitness. It was inscribed on a board and when Jesus was marched from the Praetorium, Pilate's judgement hall, if custom was followed, he had to carry it to the place of execution, Skull Hill; or it was hung round his neck. It spelled out his crime. It read 'Jesus of Nazareth the King of the Jews'. And when the cross was hauled into the upright position the board was nailed to the top of it. It looked like an inscription on a tombstone.

Now Pilate hated the Jews. To him they were unruly religious fanatics and he was particularly incensed at this Passover time because they had trapped him into condemning to death a man whom he considered innocent and who did not look in the least like a criminal. He burned to get his own back on the Jews for this defeat. He would label this Jesus of Nazareth broken on the cross as the King of the Jews. He hoped they would get the message. This is the only king they deserved to have, a dead one. They did get the message and it infuriated them. Did someone leak to the chief priests what Pilate was writing on that board? So it would appear. Storming into his presence they ordered 'Do not write "Jesus of Nazareth the King of the Jews" but that he said he was King of the Jews'. They were afraid that when that board was eventually nailed up as a title over the cross on which Jesus hung, sticking up there by the roadside north of Jerusalem where the many passers-by would read it they could not be sure what would be the consequences, perhaps a popular uprising. But Pilate was in no mood for compromise. He had had enough of this shady business. He barked out three words: 'Quod scripsi, scripsi', 'What I have written I have written'. So the board was taken by Jesus, or by some other, and put up over his crucifixion. It was his label. It was his title.

Now was this title correct? Was Jesus King of the Jews? Did Jesus ever make this claim? We go back to the Jewish Council bringing Jesus before Pilate after their condemnation of him. They brought three charges—perverting the nation, forbidding to give tribute to Caesar, and saying that he himself is Christ, a King. Pilate fastened on the word 'King' but as he looked at Jesus he knew he was out of his depth. Jesus did not look in the least like a king in the normal sense nor anything like a claimant to national power. He carried no weapons. He had no band of rebels. And when he put the straight question to Jesus, 'Are you the King of the Jews', he received no straight answer, because of course in the sense of being the Messiah, the Christ, he was the King, not only of the Jews but of all peoples. Such spiritual subtleties however were outside Pilate's Roman legal way of thinking. The entire situation baffled him and irritated him. He would wash his hands of it, and if the title 'King of the Jews' angered the Jews, well and good, he would anger them. And so he bent over his slave with the board and writing materials at hand ordering him to write those words 'Jesus of Nazareth the King of the Jews', what was more, so that every passer-by could read them, write them in the form of a trilingual label spelled out in Latin, Greek and Hebrew, cause what trouble it might, Pilate no longer cared.

So Jesus was crucified as a king. To that extent his label, Pilate's label for him, was correct, but not a national sovereign, not in the remotest sense an aspiring national overlord; he was crucified as the Messianic King. The cross on Skull Hill was the place where *the Christ* was crucified.

2 THREE LANGUAGES

And now I would like you to imagine yourself one of the passers-by on the road leading into Jerusalem. You see the cross, you are unable not to see it. It is put there to be seen. A macabre spectacle. You see the title, you read the label. Three lines roughly of equal length despite the three languages. Latin first, it would be, the Romans were everywhere, they clamped down on everything, had 'a finger in every pie', and were hated for it. Next Greek. Everybody above the level of the labouring class could read Greek and spoke it after a fashion. The bottom line of the title was written in Hebrew characters, or more strictly speaking Aramaic, the native everyday tongue of the Jewish people.

So the crucifixion was not hushed up. It was made blatantly public. And not only did it take place in a land where East and West meet, it was labelled in the languages of the three great world cultures of the time; Latin the language of administration, Greek the language of culture and Hebrew (or Aramaic) the language of religion. No part of civilized life therefore was blocked off from making a judgement on the crucifixion of Christ. All would sooner or later have to reckon with what took place at Golgotha at least with fleeting interest if not with a measure of serious reflection. The crucifixion was of universal significance. It was involved with the world in general, not simply with the world of religion. The label on the cross will not allow piety to claim it exclusively for its own, it has something to say to the community's administration, something to say to the culture which is built upon it, something to say to organized religion. The crucifixion is of worldwide significance. It stands as the criterion of human nature in all its varied and various manifestations. The original cross was not set up in a cloister but out on the world's frontier where cultures clash sharpened by language barriers. The cross points up our perennial differences.

3 CHRIST IS KING

We go back to Pilate's title, 'Jesus of Nazareth the King of the Jews'. The Latin word for king is *rex*, a word of stirring significance in the story of mankind. Of all the unlikely places it found its way to the top of the cross of Jesus and there at the instigation of none other than Pontius Pilate who crucified him. 'Take him and crucify him yourselves', he shouted to the Jewish priests baying for his blood. And when people skirted the repulsive crucifixion spectacle by the roadside they read the emotive word—*Rex*. Pilate indeed put it there out of malice though not for the victim. What he wrote was *Rex Judaeorum*, King of the Jews; but many true words get spoken when other motives are in operation. Christ *is* King. The fourth gospel, in particular, telling the story of the crucifixion, words the narrative so as to bring out the royalty of the victim.

Christ is King. A king is supreme. He is set apart. And he has authority. What he says is final. So it was with Jesus the Incarnate Christ in Galilee and Judaea. No sooner did he stand up to preach in Capernaum but his hearers were 'astonished at his teaching' (I am quoting from Mark 1.22) 'for he taught them as one having authority'. But the phrase 'the King and his subjects' is wholly inappropriate with reference to Christ. He subjects no one to his kingship. There is no compulsion in his sovereignty. Everyone is left free either to accept his rule or to reject it, either to bow the knee in humble submission, or to crucify him in angry revolt. But all who grant him the title *Rex* must live by his teaching, his example and his commands and seek his forgiveness in failure and the power to try again.

So we choose our King and then abide by our choice. The situation is not unlike that in a business concern where a managing director is appointed from among the employees after consultation with them. They may not approve of him, they may not like him, in which case they are at liberty to leave the firm, there is no compulsion to stay, but if they stay they are expected to follow his directions. Now a great deal depends on the quality and ability of the man, or woman, appointed. In much of the recent discussion going on, some of it acrimonious, about the examination successes of various schools, the point has been made over and over again that the quality of a school depends in the first place, and almost in the last place too, on the kind of Head who is appointed, not on the buildings, the playing facilities and the cash available, important though these are. With a good Head, with a good managing director, chaos is unknown, a bad spirit is not in evidence, and in the relatively happy atmosphere examination success and productivity rise. The rule then, and there certainly is a rule, is a beneficent one.

Something like this is how Christ *operates* (I said 'operates') as King. We are his willing subjects or we are not his subjects at all. If we are, the outcome is an ordered life and a productive life. Christians always have something to show for their allegiance, sometimes much, sometimes little, but always something; and where there is allegiance there is no chaos, and where there is no chaos there is achievement and the inner contentment that goes with it.

Christ bears the label *Rex*, the King, at the place of his greatest achievement. Let us acknowledge him as our King. There will be achievements on our part to show.

11

THE GATE OF DEATH

Mary Magdalene and the other Mary were there, sitting opposite the sepulchre.

MATTHEW 27.61 (RSV)

Last week in one of the 'quality newspapers', so called, there appeared an article on bereavement accompanied by an eye-catching picture of a Victorian lady and gentleman wearing the black clothes that were almost *de rigeur* in their day as evidence of mourning. All this has gone, including the modest black armband even the poor managed. And nowadays at funeral services in church it is not uncommon for very little dark clothing to be in evidence. Signs of mourning in today's world are out. Is it that we no longer care about the loss of anyone? Is it that we are scared of being dubbed morbid? Or is it that we reckon the Easter Gospel of resurrection should do away with sadness, and funeral services become instead thanksgivings with triumphal music and nothing approaching a lament?

Now the writer of the newspaper article to which I have referred set out a reasoned argument to show that the abandonment of mourning, replacing it with a kind of forced fortitude, drives grief deep down into the human psyche, risking psychological damage. That way come nervous breakdowns, neuroses, depressions and other personal complications. The wearing of mourning will not of course act as a magic palliative but it will exteriorize the tension which, whether we admit it or not, is brought about by bereavement. I am in no position to make recommendations about clothing but this I will say, and must say: there is no support to be had from Christ himself for the idea that the exhibition of sorrow in bereavement is out of place in view of the resurrection. When at the grave of his friend Lazarus, who had just died, the mourners turned to look at Jesus they saw tears streaming down his face and could not but remark 'See how he loved him!' and that immediately before he proceeded to raise Lazarus to life again (John 11.33–36). And when he himself was crucified and dead, would he not expect tears to be streaming down the faces of those who loved him? All four gospels provide circumstantial accounts of the burial. It is not glossed over. I invite you therefore to weigh what happened.

1 THE WOMEN AT THE CRUCIFIXION

I begin with Mary his mother. There is a verse in John 19 about the crucifixion scene which I can hardly believe. 'So the soldiers did this. But standing by the cross of Jesus were his mother, and his mother's sister, Mary the wife of Clopas, and Mary Magdalene.' The mind shrinks from the thought of the jibes, insults and coarse insinuations the four women must have suffered from the soldiers as they stood there. Remember Mary Magdalene was a young woman and no relative of the crucified. But they stood there as close by the cross as was allowed. Mary stood there. How she did it is beyond my comprehension, for there is nothing like the bond between mother and child, mother and son, no matter what the interval of time or alteration of circumstance. When the soldiers crucified Jesus they crucified his mother. And yet she stood there. My guess is that when the onlookers had wearied of their vulgarities even they were struck by this most uncommon sight in their world of a woman torn with grief yet not tearing her clothes, dishevelling her hair or wallowing on the ground. She stood there and three other women stood with her. People talk readily today and angrily, about the dignity of woman. I ask you: did it ever rise higher than when Mary stood silently by as her Son was being tortured to death, a 'sword piercing her own soul' as years before Simeon in the temple prophesied it would?

Then Jesus saw her. When anyone is in terrible physical agony they are aware of very little else but pain, but moments of elucidation do break in to the blackness. Momentarily Jesus was conscious of his mother standing there and by her side one disciple, her nephew John. He saw her close to breaking point and bade John take her home, which he did. If we have any imagination left we can visualize this young man and this older woman on his arm toiling back into the city where he left her, poor Mary, and returned to the crucifixion.

This is is what John then witnessed. The great cry of victory from Jesus; then his dying commendation in prayer to his heavenly Father; then the smashing with a mallet of the legs of the two crucified with Jesus, making certain they were dead and their bodies ready for disposal;

51

then the checking that Jesus was already dead and so his legs remained unbroken; nevertheless a soldier jabbed a spear into his side to make sure. The account in St John says there flowed out blood and water and it seems to attach importance to this. I must be honest; I read this simply as evidence that Jesus really was dead before being taken down from the cross. Some read it as evidence that even in death corruption had no power over his body and point to Acts 2.31. Again some see in the blood and water flowing from Jesus' pierced side a reference to the two sacraments of the Eucharist and Baptism. If I must be called an agnostic at this point, I must, but a reverent one.

Then Joseph of Arimathea, a secret disciple of Jesus, arrived with permission from Pilate to take away the body, then Nicodemus with a mixture of myrrh and aloes to fold into the linen cloths in which they would bury him. Together they moved off to the garden nearby where was the tomb they intended to use. It was a pathetic little funeral procession and at the end of it a tiny group of women. And when the burial was over two of them 'were still sitting there opposite the sepulchre', Mary Magdalene and one called 'the other Mary'.

At this point there comes into my mind that moving sculpture called the Pietà by Michelangelo at the entrance of St Peter's in Rome. The New Testament tells us nothing about Mary, the mother of Jesus taking the dead body of her Son lovingly in her arms after the crucifixion; but now, back in Jerusalem and alone, she must have done just this in heart and mind, weeping all the time.

Jesus and his mother must have been very close. Son of God though he was she brought him up. Was the timbre of their voices similar? And something about their facial expression? For thirty years in Nazareth they were together. They talked together, shared problems together and prayed together. He must have shared his thinking with her formulating perhaps what came to be those profound yet homely parables. Was there ever a woman so educated as Mary? And she knew her Son had a special destiny as is evident by his remark to her at the wedding in Cana of Galilee 'My hour has not yet come' (John 2.4). But her motherly instinct to seek to control his mission had to be checked on this and a later occasion (Mark 3.31f.). Blood relationship was not to give her what the Germans call *Amt*, office, in the working out of the ministry of her Son. She did not see him again after she left the crucifixion site. There was no resurrection appearance to her.

2 DEATH AS A GATE

I have dealt with the death and burial of Jesus in some detail because the New Testament accounts do so. It could be said that the reason for this fullness is to leave no doubts that he really died by crucifixion. He did not merely swoon and later revive. So the resurrection was real. This is sound reasoning but there is more to be said. Jesus entered into his risen life 'through the grave and gate of death' as the Collect for Easter Even in the Book of Common Prayer puts it. In Genesis 5.24 we read, 'Enoch walked with God; and he was not, for God took him'. And then this in the letter to the Hebrews (11.5): 'By faith Enoch was taken up so that he should not see death; and he was not found, because God had taken him'. Did not Jesus walk with God? But he was not 'taken'. He entered the risen life 'through the grave and gate of death' as we must. He used no back door into heaven, no quick passage. The story of the Ascension in the New Testament follows the death and burial, it does not dispense with either. Jesus went all the way we have to go from the cradle to the grave. The incarnation was complete, nothing short-circuited.

All this presents us with a new way of conceiving death. It is a gate. It was a gate for Jesus into the risen life. It will be a gate for us who unite ourselves to him by faith into the risen life. Let us be honest. It is not an attractive gate. In a way it is an ugly gate. And the people who (please God) will stand by when we go through may well be weeping; and when we have gone, mourn the loss, but since Christ has died and has risen death is not a blank wall any more, it is not a dead end, it is a gate, and on the other side is life and light and immortality. No wonder the early Church never erected a shrine in the place where he was buried.

3 THE MINISTRY AT THE GATE

I began this sermon with a reference to mourning customs. We shall be wise to be careful about these but all in whom is something of the Christian spirit have more to do than mourn, though the weeping with those who weep is a ministry in itself. We have to do all we can to ease people's passage through the gate, physically, mentally and spiritually. Thank God for the Hospice Movement. Everything to do with dying, the grave, and the gate of death must be carried out with dignity. And here, it seems to me, women have a distinctive role. At both ends of human life, birth and death, they are there. Yes, 'death is swallowed up in victory'. This is the good news of the Gospel, but before the victory there is the battle. Blessed are all they who help us there. And if there are around us ministering women, ministering 'angels' whom God in his mercy provides, I wonder, yes I wonder if he has ministering angels to help us on *the other side* of the gate when we pass into the (at first) strangeness of heaven. Roman Catholics will not find this difficult to believe. I am not a Roman Catholic, though my mother came from a Roman Catholic family, so maybe I have a trace of Roman Catholicism in my blood, I would like to believe as they believe in this. I would like to believe that there are ministering angels on both sides of the grave and gate of death even if the angels on this side have to be written with inverted commas.

12

WHERE WAS GOD IN THE CRUCIFIXION?

Why standest thou so far off, O Lord : and hidest thy face in the needful time of trouble?

PSALM 10.1 (BCP)

I wonder if you have ever had the experience after a journey in the dark arriving at a house where you are to stay and being shown up to your room. You don't know quite where you are. You draw the curtains back and peer out into the blackness but cannot make out what you see. Are those black shapes out there trees or houses? But there is a rustling as of leaves. So trees perhaps. But is there a road nearby? You think you hear a car engine. And then what could be footfalls. You pull the curtains across and go to bed dissatisfied. You don't know where you are. In the morning after sunrise you hasten to look out again. How different! What was puzzling now has meaning, not completely but more than enough to give you satisfaction. You go about your day. I want to suggest that the relationship between Good Friday and Easter is something like that. Easter does not take Good Friday away any more than the sunrise took that scene outside the window away. Nor does Easter diminish it. The sunrise enhances the view outside the window. So Easter with respect to the crucifixion, and that permanently.

1 THE ABSENCE OF GOD

First of all I wish to emphasize how dark is the crucifixion, how puzzling, even menacing. God is not obvious there, rather the reverse. From all we can see, God was absent from Calvary. There was no compassion, only cruelty, hate, gloating and callousness. Yes, some tears on the part of a handful of women standing afar off, and by the crosses a jar of sour wine for the victims, a tiny index of residual mercy. Nothing else. No angel. No miracle, no supporting band of disciples even at the back of the gaping crowd. Jesus was alone, man-forsaken, apparently God-forsaken. 'My God, my God why hast thou forsaken me?' was his terrible cry. 'Why standest thou so far off, O Lord : and hidest thy face in the needful time of trouble?'

In the crucifixion Jesus goes out (or should we say down?) to where apparently—I said apparently—God is not. But the Psalmist did say 'If I go down to hell, thou art there also' (139). In the world as we know it Jesus was not the only one to go out there or down there. As we sit here there are people slowly dying in labour camps; and prisoners in solitary confinement cells shivering with the knowledge that soon their torturers will arrive; and emaciated men, women and children raking over the rubbish tips in the back streets of Calcutta for something to eat. The list could be prolonged. 'Why standest thou so far off, O Lord : and hidest thy face in the needful time of trouble?'

I appreciate why some scholars hurry to the crucifixion with theories of the atonement; rightly they wish to give it meaning for us today but we shall not enter into the reality of the crucifixion unless first we stand before it with nothing to say, it is so awful. I remember vividly one November morning coming away from that grim Holocaust memorial in Jerusalem with a scholarly friend and sitting on a bench in the warm autumn sunshine. We were not insensitive. We were too sensitive to speak. This is why I am half reluctant to preach on Good Friday. I only want to stand again, as it were, at Golgotha and let what I see, or try to see, a horror scene where God is not, sink into my consciousness. 'Why standest thou so far off, O Lord : and hidest thy face in the needful time of trouble?'

This is what the crucifixion says first of all. There are times and places where atheism seems justified and it is one of the most stunning features of Christianity that its central symbol says this. There are of course atheists who are atheists because they wish to appear sophisticated and far above the simplicities (as they see them) of faith. And there are atheists who cannot be bothered to think through the complexities of human existence. There are also atheists who have been broken by what has happened to them and what they have witnessed. They have been driven to atheism and it hurts, supplying no healing balm. On Good Friday Jesus went to that kind of place where atheism is born. 'Why standest thou so far off, O Lord : and hidest thy face in the needful time of trouble?' I find this so stunning I can only just believe it, but this is the message I want to whisper on Good Friday to atheists who may think it has nothing for them—Christ went where you are.

2 GOD IS REVEALED IN WEAKNESS

And now the pertinent question. Where was God in the crucifixion? Why was God so far off? Why does he seem so far off? The straight answer is, God was there in the crucifixion but we do not recognize him because we find it hard to believe that God is manifested in weakness, indeed the very suggestion seems downright stupid.

This is our trouble, we do not in the first place even look for God in the crucifixion, we begin with an abstract definition of God instead. We say God equals power. Is he not the Almighty? Nothing is beyond his strength, his wisdom, his ingenuity. And with this in mind we expect miracles in his way of working, stirring events and wonders; and frequently are disappointed, if not incensed, because we do not often see them; tragedies occur, calamities and hideous persecution of men and women by men and women; and God does nothing, or so it appears, to stop them. So if there is no God of power in evidence, then we must conclude there is no God at all.

Or if we do not begin our reasoning about God as equivalent to power we begin by thinking of him in abstract terms as truth, beauty and goodness. This is the philosophical approach, and great names are attached to it. What however we reach this way for all the intellectual ingenuity, and it is formidable, is 'the first cause' or 'the underlying principle' or 'the sum total of existence'. We have not by this approach encountered the real God, not the God of the Bible who is depicted in personal terms (which is not to say he is a person), one who speaks, acts and cares for people. If however we persist with intellectual abstractions we shall certainly not see God in the crucifixion, he was not only far off, he was not there. If God equals power the crucifixion is an embarrassment for there we meet one called the Son of God powerless, pitifully weak and performing no miracle even to extricate himself from the ordeal, and no one steps forward to perform one on his behalf. There are no angels, no encouraging voices from heaven, only jeering cries from the ground. The cross stands as the epitome of weakness.

St Paul faced this head on. He categorically rejected human wisdom as the way to know the real God. He put the matter plainly in his letter to the Corinthians who prided themselves on their Greek philosophy. 'But we', he wrote, 'preach Christ crucified, a stumbling block to Jews and folly to Greeks but to those who are called, both Jews and Greeks, Christ the power of God and the wisdom of God.'

So there is power in God and wisdom in God but they are manifested in weakness. Unlike their counterpart in the world they are not employed to force submission. Domination is foreign to God's way, yet remarkable results follow. Has there ever been any event so powerful as the crucifixion to change men and women, and thereby alter the course of history?

3 GOD ACTED IN THE CRUCIFIXION

And so we have to turn to the crucifixion and not from the crucifixion, counting God as absent from it, if we would know him. It is there that he is manifested, revealed in and through weakness. Yes, it takes some believing; it seems contrary to common sense, upside-down thinking, or in the more dignified wording of St Paul's letter to the Corinthians 'folly', but to the cross we must go in order to know God, not only revealing his nature but also actually in action on behalf of mankind.

Revelation by itself is not enough. Let me put it to you. What would you think of a couple, a model couple in many respects, never quarrelling, caring for each other and for their two bright and healthy children? They set them an example of what marital happiness can be. But they let their children go their own way. They took no interest in their schooling, never accompanied them on a holiday, never even an evening out together as a family to an entertainment. And if you think this picture overdrawn I have to tell you I saw this happening over a period of time. So I make my point. A revelation of goodness is not enough, there has to be action, indeed there cannot be a revelation of goodness without action and that on behalf of others.

So what was God doing in the crucifixion? He was making a revelation of himself through a supreme example of self-sacrifice. And those who behold it sympathetically are moved to mend their ways and be saved from self-centredness and selfishness, the grounds of many troubles. But is a revelation strong enough to wrest us from self-centredness? Is not the human will flawed so that it cannot pull itself up? Can we go on then and say that in the crucifixion God was actually breaking the power of sin so that it no longer has dominion? But where? Only in the hearts and minds of those who believe, or also in all men and women everywhere? What about the words of the Consecration Prayer in the Communion Service (BCP), 'who made there by his one oblation of himself once offered a full, perfect, and sufficient sacrifice, oblation, and satisfaction, for the sins of the *whole world*'? So the crucifixion is God's work for the whole of mankind. Can we believe this? The Church believes it. Each one of us must make up our minds where we stand. And if we find the grasping of all this difficult or beyond our ability, then ally with the Church *without understanding*. It is the place of safety. 'God was in Christ, reconciling *the world* unto himself' (2 Corinthians 5.19). This is where God was in the crucifixion.

13

THE NEW HUMANITY

But a certain Samaritan, as he journeyed, came where he was.

LUKE 10.33

The subject I am handling today was pinpointed for me by a friend's remark in the course of a general conversation. He said 'The incarnation is summarized for me in the text, "he came where he was" '. I thought about this on my way home in the train: 'he came where he was'. It refers to the Good Samaritan, as we call him, in the story which Jesus told, and how he, seeing by the roadside the wretched, bruised and broken victim of an assault by robbers, stripped of all his possessions, almost of life itself, did not 'pass by on the other side' as did the priest and Levite but came where he was to succour, and that liberally. The full text reads: 'But a certain Samaritan, as he journeyed, came where he was: and when he saw him, he had compassion on him, and went to him, and bound up his wounds, pouring in oil and wine, and set him on his own beast, and brought him to an inn, and took care of him'.

1 THE CLIMAX OF THE INCARNATION

This is the thought I bring to your consideration. The crucifixion is the climax, the fulfilment of the Incarnation, God becoming flesh and dwelling among us.

Certainly he came to teach, to set us an example of Godly life, to heal, and in his choice of the twelve apostles to lay the foundation of the Christian Church but, to crown all, he came to be where the greater part of humanity is and always has been, the pit of deprivation, poverty, pain and hopelessness. He came where humanity is. For him it meant a place called Golgotha, the Place of the Skull where they crucified him. There he was seen down as low as any man could be, down with the dregs, out-casts and pain-soaked people of the world, stripped even of common decency, dying slowly in public, a thing of gloating fascination for the coarsest of human instincts.

So my question, Where shall we find God? In churches and temples? Yes. In the homes and lives of the faithful servants of God? Yes. Among people in all walks of life, some in palaces, some in positions of leadership in Church and state, executives, technicians, athletes, housewives, nurses? Yes. But we must be ready to look among the outcasts and broken. 'He came where he was.' This is what the crucifixion, gaunt and ugly, stands to tell us. God identifies with those for whom no one cares. If at some time, perhaps as a tourist, you have been shown a dungeon deep within a fortress where prisoners were chained till they died, you may have noticed how often crosses had been scratched on the walls. Clearly these wretched men knew what the crucifixion was saying; 'God if no one else, is with us. We are not forgotten.' The cross was their only hope.

2 THE AUTHENTIC CHRISTIAN MINISTER

And now this. The message of the Christian gospel is unlikely to be heard unless the messenger is willing to go where the needy are.

In 1985 there was published in a book by Dominique Lapierre the story of a young Polish priest called Stephen Kovalski who felt his ministry lay among the poor of Calcutta. On arrival there he called on the bishop, an Anglo-Indian of about fifty, who wore a white cassock, a purple skull-cap and a majestic manner, and lived in a beautiful colonial-style house surrounded by a vast garden. Hearing that Kovalski wished to work among the poor he introduced him to a priest whose parish lay in the most deprived part of the city but whose church was beautifully furnished and equipped even with electric fans to keep the worshippers cool. With a paunch beneath an immaculate cassock this priest looked askance at Kovalski in his jeans and baseball boots and passed him on to an assistant who conducted him to the nearby slum of Amard Nagar, one of the oldest in Calcutta, wedged in between a railway embankment and two factories. Seventy thousand people lived there on a piece of land only three times the size of a football field. There was not one tree, and no flowers, butterflies or birds except vultures and crows. Here air pollution killed one member of every family; leprosy, tuberculosis and dysentery abounded. Life expectancy was one of the lowest in the world.

61

This is where Kovalski rented a windowless hovel with a beaten earth floor, no furniture, no electricity and no running water. Near the door was an overflowing open drain and over it on a tiny platform, a tea shop. The neighbours took time to believe that Kovalski really was a priest but when at last they did they brought him a mat, a bucket and a lamp for his new home. This minister of Christ really had come where these crushed people were and the sight gave them an entirely new picture of the God in whose service this young priest lived his life. He had come where they were.

It is most unlikely that any one of us will feel called to the slums of Calcutta as was this young Polish priest, or to any place like it, but the lesson is plain and clear. The Christian Church and its preaching of the Gospel will not be authentic if it stands aloof from people who for one reason or another are down in the slough of despond. Their suffering may be due to illness, material poverty, a broken marriage, anti-Semitism, racial hatred or sheer ignorance. The minister of Christ crucified must be willing to go wherever there is pain and for whatever reason.

3 THE OLD AND THE NEW HUMANITY

I come back to the crucifixion. In due time we may have to wrestle with it theologically but before we do let us see it as a disclosure of the new humanity. Here on the cross was Someone who did not hit back not even with the limited possibilities that were open to him. He did not curse and swear pouring out whatever vituperation could be spat out like the two crucified with him, one on either side. They were rebels against all that constituted ordered society imperfect as it was and always is in every age. Jesus was different and not only from the violent law-breakers but from those who apparently conformed. They stood around the crucifixion, some taking part in the crucifying, some merely watching, some mouthing their satisfaction, among whom, sad to say, were priests and lawyers. So at the crucifixion the two humanities are vividly disclosed over against each other, the new humanity, the man of the cross, praying 'Father forgive them' and, gathered around, the old humanity shaking their fists.

I am not saying the new humanity is seen nowhere else among mankind, not in the history of the world and in no religions other than the

Christian. In our text for this sermon we saw it in a Samaritan. There are some magnificent disclosures in unexpected places. What I am saying is that the disclosure of the new humanity over against the old is *focused* in the crucifixion. It comes to be seen in those who look there in faith and who live by what they see. And their way of life spreads out, sometimes with a bright light, often with an indifferent light; but always the new humanity when true to itself turns away from the old attitudes of rebellion, hatred, cursing and lies. Conflicts remain. The old humanity has a way of rising up at times seeking to crush the new, but the new must persevere. This perseverance is called the way of the Cross both for the individual Christian and for Christ's Church.

In preaching the crucifixion which has been my aim in these sermons I have been at pains to portray the event. We must begin with what happened. This history is fundamental in the Christian faith but it is not a history that has passed away. It is not over and done with now. The crucifixion stands as a perpetual disclosure of what humanity is and can be. It is also a reminder that there is suffering in God always. It is even more than a disclosure it is *action* on behalf of mankind. To this we shall have to give our attention and try to see how, for it is not obvious. This much we must notice now, indeed we cannot close our eyes to what is a fact, the crucifixion does not take away suffering. It shows God in Christ *sharing our suffering*. So the refrain spoken in the Eucharist, the *Agnus Dei* is not 'O Lamb of God that taketh away the suffering of the world' but 'O Lamb of God that taketh away the sins of the world'. Can we really believe this ' . . . taketh away the sins *of the world*'? We shall need to wrestle with this. For the moment let us be satisfied to keep hold of the crucifixion in our faith and not let it go. There is no extremity of life to which it has nothing to say.

Let me end with a story. It is told by a German called Hans Lang and is about an old Russian. 'His presence was always a comfort in those days full of struggle and death. When I got to know him he was already eighty years old, at one time the owner of an estate, happily married and the father of seven sons and five daughters. For twenty-seven years he was banished with his family to Siberia. His wife died there, and seven children. The other five children he lost in the war. When I asked him what he looked for in life now, he answered, "I have had many blessings. I have experienced the heights and depths of life. I have nothing else now only this." Then he thrust his hand into his pocket and, wrapped in a handkerchief, pulled out a crucifix. "This is all that is left to me now. It is nothing—but on the other hand it is everything." ' When I read this in the *Neukirchener Kalender* (1991) the words of Charles Wesley's hymn came into my mind,

> Other refuge have I none;
> Hangs my helpless soul on thee;
> Leave, ah! leave me not alone,
> Still support and comfort me.
> All my trust on thee is stayed,
> All my help from thee I bring;
> Cover my defenceless head
> With the shadow of thy wing.

14

AMAZING GRACE

And now, brethren, I know that you acted in ignorance, as did also your rulers. But what God foretold by the mouth of all the prophets, that his Christ should suffer, he thus fulfilled. Repent therefore, and turn again, that your sins may be blotted out, that times of refreshing may come from the presence of the Lord.

ACTS 3.17–19 (RSV)

A few years ago I listened to a woman giving a lecture, to some ordination candidates on bereavement—how it affects people, what to think about it and how to face it. She worked in a hospice. I was impressed by both what she said and the way she said it. Bereavement hurts. It hurts most where love is strongest. And if it happens to strike on a special day such as Christmas Day or the anniversary of a wedding the pain is nearly unbearable.

1 GRIEF DISPELLED

With this in mind I wonder if any Sabbath—a day of rejoicing and not gloom in the Jewish tradition—was ever more black than that which the disciples and friends of Jesus endured on the Sabbath immediately following the day of the crucifixion. They had expected to be keeping the Passover with praise and thanksgiving in company with thousands upon thousands of pilgrims come to Jerusalem for that purpose, and there they were bereft of the man they loved. And not only that but they were tormented with the nightmarish memory of him strung up on that hideous gibbet, an object of revulsion to all who passed by; and as if that were not sufficient to crush their spirits the thought that all hope of his Messiahship was gone for ever. The Messiah could not die, but Jesus *was dead*.

St Luke has a story illustrative of their utter dismay. Two people

65

walking along a road outside the city joined by a third to whom they said 'We had hoped', but not now, 'we had hoped that he was the one to redeem Israel'. Their blank despair however was suddenly wiped away. It was sudden. It was unexpected. The resurrection of Christ was the cause. Please note the resurrection was not an ecclesiastical doctrine hammered out by theologians over a period of decades. It happened overnight. And it gave birth to the Church, the Church did not give birth to the idea of the resurrection. There was no Church till after the resurrection had taken place. And it took away the crushing despair of that black Sabbath following the crucifixion. In its place was joy if not excitement. Christ was risen. Christ is risen. Jesus is Lord.

2 THE CRUCIFIXION NEVER TO BE FORGOTTEN

Now what Easter does not mean is that the crucifixion is forgotten, rubbed out, blotted out from memory, a horrible thing over and done with for ever. It was a battle that was fought on Good Friday, a battle on behalf of the whole world and it was won! Easter is the day for celebrating that victory and for keeping it in the forefront of our minds and gradually to grasp the benefits which flow from it. A poor illustration admittedly, but an illustration, might be the battle of Waterloo fought in 1815 which changed the face of Europe. The consequences which flow from victories take time to be realized, so it was with Good Friday. Time is required to grasp the implications which is why the crucifixion has to be preached.

No, Good Friday is not blotted out by Easter. It is never blotted out. In St John's gospel is a story driving this home. The disciples in the evening of that first Easter Day had locked themselves together behind closed doors 'for fear of the Jews' as the record says. Evidently they were not sure they would not be arrested as was Jesus and perhaps be crucified. Then suddenly there was Jesus standing among them with the most familiar, almost pedestrian of all greetings, 'Peace be with you', almost like saying 'Good evening'. This sermon is not the time for me to talk about the resurrection appearances, what I wish is to draw your attention to what Jesus did after his greeting—he showed them his hands and his side. They saw the wound marks of his crucifixion. Was this for the purpose of identification?—this really was Jesus standing among them. No doubt it was but for something else even more important. The risen

Christ, the glorified Christ, Christ the Lord, bears for ever those wound marks, *stigmata*, as they are often called. This is the point to be grasped. It is the crucified Christ who is Lord, the crucified and risen Christ to which we might add the crucified, risen and ascended Christ, the Christ in glory. He always bears the wound marks of his passion. No wonder then the crucifixion is stamped on the Christian memory for ever, it is never superseded, not even in eternity. The cross therefore is the permanent sign of the whole assembly of the Church. It marks where the church is.

3 NO REVENGE

The crucifixion is no ground for revenge. We return to our text, Acts 3.17: 'And now, brethren, I know that you acted in ignorance, as did also your rulers', words attributed to St Peter addressing the crowds who came running to him in the one of the temple porches after he had healed a lame man. There followed straight-speaking words. We might even say 'he pulled no punches'. Listen: 'The God of Abraham, Isaac and Jacob, the God of our fathers, has given the highest honour to his servant Jesus whom you delivered up and denied in the presence of Pilate when he had decided to release him. But you denied the Holy and Righteous One, and asked for a murderer to be granted to you, and killed the Author of Life, whom God raised from the dead. To this we are witnesses.' Did Peter's hearers flinch when they heard themselves charged as guilty men? And what a charge! Killing the Prince of Life! But then followed this. We can scarcely believe it. No doubt those hanging on the words spoken could scarcely believe them: 'And now, brethren, I know that you acted in ignorance as did also your rulers'.

This is extraordinary. There is not even a breath of revenge. No call for the guilty men to be brought to justice. No cry for God to intervene. How unlike our modern situation. As soon as some calamity or tragedy occurs in the modern world there is a hasty clamouring for a law case, a demand for those thought to be responsible to be deprived of offices and compensation to be paid to the victims. This may be right. What is hard to imagine is any newspaper article daring to write 'They did what they did in ignorance, as did also their rulers'. But this is precisely what St Peter said about that monumental miscarriage of justice—the crucifixion. 'They did it in ignorance.' There was

67

absolutely no call for revenge by Peter the chief apostle of the early Church.

If only the Church from its beginnings till this day had followed St Peter in this. But little time elapsed before Christians, yes, some Christians, stirred up hatred against the Jews as the crucifiers of the Messiah, fuelling a bitter conflict between Church and Synagogue. And this spilled over into the general attitude towards the Jews throughout Christendom with some notable exceptions. They were treated shamefully, indeed anti-Semitism became the shame of the so-called Christian nations and is not dead yet. As a result the crucifix became one of the most loathed objects. And injury was added to insult when the tortures of the Inquisition were carried out in its presence. So the message of the crucifixion was turned upside down and the cross became a symbol of hate. This is not the way to preach the crucifixion. If only the words of the chief apostle St Peter had been heeded. 'I know that in ignorance you did it.' His complete absence from any spirit of revenge would have changed history, ugly history.

How can we account for this remarkable statement by the apostle, made in Jerusalem and very shortly after the crucifixion itself? I do not know. How could I know? But I believe the reason must be sought in the words of Jesus himself. When he lay on the ground on Skull Hill and the four Roman soldiers were nailing his hands to the transom of the cross he prayed these words, 'Father, forgive them for they know not what they do'. What amazing grace is this! And what an extraordinary simple basis for forgiveness! We can hardly believe it. Certainly those Christians with complicated theories of atonement can hardly believe it. Some have even suggested that Jesus did not pray the words, they have been put into his mouth, for there was no one at the nailing operation to report them. But this makes the unknown originator even more unbelievable. Could it not be that somehow what Jesus himself said reached the ears of Peter, sank into his consciousness, was quickened by the Holy Spirit on the day of Pentecost and became one of the hallmarks ever after of the Christian attitude to sinners—forgiveness? All this should act to temper any harsh theories of the atonement which in our theological moods we might be tempted to elaborate, writing off what St Peter said as belonging to the early, if not naive, thinking of the early days of the Christian Church.

4 GOD AT WORK IN THE CRUCIFIXION

Once more we return to the text briefly to point out three additional statements by St Peter. Having said that his hearers and their rulers acted in ignorance in crucifying Jesus he added 'But what God foretold by the mouths of all the prophets, that his Christ should suffer, he thus fulfilled'. In other words, God was in the crucifixion and not simply man's evil deeds. God overruled. He is at work even when all seems at its darkest and most repulsive. This does not mean that no further action is called for. Wrongdoing, even if carried out ignorantly at the time, demands repentance, and repentance, turning again (could we say 'turning over a new life'?) is the way sins are blotted out. And the outcome? 'Times of refreshing from the presence of the Lord.' What a lovely phrase this is—times of refreshing! It conjures up thoughts of a blissful holiday in the fresh air and sunshine. What a remarkable way to bring to an end a sermon on the crucifixion. Perhaps Psalm 126 could appropriately be sung here, 'When the Lord turned again the captivity of Sion : then were we like unto them that dream. Then was our mouth filled with laughter : and our tongue with joy.' All because of amazing grace, God's grace.

15

THE CRUCIFIXION AND THE FORGIVENESS OF SINS

Repent then and turn to God, so that your sins may be wiped out.
ACTS 3.19 (NEB)

On Saturday 7 December 1991 I was astonished on picking up a news-paper, granted it was what is commonly called a 'quality' paper, but I was astonished to see that the leading article was entirely devoted to the subject of forgiveness. This was because a mother whose teenage daughter at Oxford had been strangled to death by a jealous lover and hidden under the floorboards in her lodgings said she *forgave him*. Her actual words were 'You have to, otherwise it eats into your life and the lives of those around you'. The article also reported the words of Mr Terry Anderson, held hostage in Beirut for more than six years: 'I am a Christian and a Catholic . . . it is required of me to forgive no matter how hard it is and I am determined to do that'. This is not what we are accustomed to hear after an injury, but rather claims for compensation and punishment for the guilty. So the article was surprising.

1 IS NOT REPENTANCE SUFFICIENT?

My subject in this sermon is the crucifixion and the forgiveness of sins. This is not a side issue. No matter how carefully and rightly I may have tried to emphasize that the crucifixion actually took place, and that Christianity rests on solid historical fact and not merely on an idea however laudable, I shall have failed to *preach* the crucifixion unless I bring it into the world of our experience, our personal experience and this means focusing on the forgiveness of sins.

I begin with the children's hymn:

> There is a green hill far away,
> Without a city wall,

> Where the dear Lord was crucified,
>   Who died to save us all.
> He died that we might be forgiven,
>   He died to make us good,
> That we might go at last to heaven,
>   Saved by his precious Blood.
>
> (Mrs C. F. Alexander)

Did he? Did 'the dear Lord' die that we might be forgiven? Could not God forgive us our sins without that horrible crucifixion? Couldn't he forgive us if we confess that we are sorry for what we have done and if we try to do better next time? Don't you, a parent, forgive your child if he/she runs to you with the words 'I'm sorry Dad, I'm sorry Mum'? Do you demand punishment first, corporal punishment? And if you can't bear to inflict it on the *naughty* child in the family do you inflict it instead on the *obedient* one because punishment has to be meted out for sins? I am speaking in simple terms, almost childish terms but I did open up the subject with a children's hymn, and by putting a question mark against the line 'he died that we might be forgiven'.

This then is the sharp point I am raising. Why is not repentance sufficient for God to forgive us our sins? He is called 'Our Father'. Why does there have to be an Atonement? Why does there have to be a crucifixion if indeed there has to be? This is the subject for our consideration.

First, let me remind you of what is perhaps the best known of all the stories Jesus told, that of the Prodigal Son; how he, the younger of two sons, asked his father to give him the inheritance money that one day would be his, and how on receiving it he wasted every penny living a fast life in a foreign country. But he came to his senses; hungry and dressed only in rags, he returned home with the abject confession, 'I have sinned against heaven and in thy sight and am no more worthy to be called thy son'; whereon his father not only forgave him but restored him to the family fellowship, and that with joyfulness. Nothing more was demanded, no price had to be paid. What more then is required for forgiveness than repentance? Why the crucifixion?

Secondly, this—if nevertheless it be maintained that the crucifixion was necessary for the forgiveness of sins, how could Christ himself forgive sins *prior* to his crucifixion? And yet we read over and over again in the first three gospels of him setting people free with the words 'Your sins are forgiven' and in the fourth gospel of the woman taken in adultery whom he let go, though with the charge not to sin again. What is more, in this and in other instances, there was not even any explicit repentance as the prelude to forgiveness, which is not to say Jesus did not read it in the heart and mind of the one he forgave. All in all, therefore, we cannot connect the forgiveness of sins *directly* with the crucifixion as if this price had to be paid before the sinner could be set free.

2 NO FORGIVENESS WITHOUT SUFFERING

But is the matter as simple as this? Is repentance all that is required? If when your child has misbehaved and says 'I'm sorry Dad, I'm sorry Mum' you reply 'That's all right, son, run off and play' will not he/she conclude that you don't much care one way or the other about what has been done? Somehow the seriousness of wrongdoing has to be brought home to the child, otherwise forgiveness is immoral. But suppose the child knows the parent has really been hurt by what has been done, suppose he/she sees the mother in tears, suppose he/she is aware that the parent is losing sleep, suppose the neighbours begin to talk, will not the offence begin to weigh heavily on the wrongdoer? And will not the words 'I'm sorry Dad, I'm sorry Mum' be drawn forth and with real *depth of feeling*?

Repentance then is far too simplistic as the ground for forgiveness. Heaven knows what agonies of heart and mind the father of the prodigal son went through when he saw his boy run away from home and land in the depths of trouble and misery. He forgave him when he came back repentant and received him into the home but the whole exercise was couched in suffering. Forgiveness is never anything else but a costly business, otherwise it is not real. There is always a cross to bear. The sins of the world, and *the sin of the world*, is the issue here. They had to involve Gethsemane and the agony of the crucifixion if the moral law was not to be left in tatters. This was the price of forgiveness.

3 THE FAMILY SETTING

I do not think we shall begin to understand this, and maybe we shall never progress very far from the beginnings of understanding anyway, but we shall not progress at all if we think of forgiveness in terms of remission of the penalty. When your boy comes home to you and says 'I'm sorry Dad', he is not asking to be let off some punishment, he may even want to suffer some punishment, what he looks for is restoration to the good friendly relations which have been broken by what he has done. Once grasp this and we shall not make the mistake of trying to interpret what was effected in the crucifixion in terms of a court room, a judge and an offender in the dock. What the offender in the dock looks for is remission of the penalty of his misdeeds, not the restoration of friendly relations with the judge, for he never had any; and as for some third party taking his punishment, it is out of the question. The only kind of setting in which we can ever begin to understand is that of a home with loving parents and child. God is our Father with whom we live and who cares for us. He does not deal with us from a basis of anger. He longs to be at peace with us, and in our heart of hearts we want to be at peace with him. He will bear what pain he must *for our wrongdoing*, what we look for is the restoration of communion with God after what we have done.

Repentance then does bring forgiveness, but genuine repentance is unlikely to be forthcoming unless we see for ourselves the hurt our wrongdoing has caused. So it is that the crucifixion, the agony of it and the humiliation of it, when we see how as part of the human family we are involved in it, moves us to repentance. This is not mere theory, there has been nothing like the cross of Christ to make men and women be sorry for their sins and to turn them from their evil ways. When we see what it cost a holy and loving Father God to forgive us our sins we repent, sometimes even in dust and ashes. So the cross is the means of our repentance, and repentance is what brings forgiveness and restoration to fellowship with him, all barriers done away. We need not then reject the line in Mrs Alexander's children's hymn, 'He died that we might be forgiven', for his dying draws us to the point of repentance whereby God will forgive us our sins.

4 THE PART THE PENITENT MUST PLAY

There is much more that could be said and no doubt ought to be said, but a phrase in the Lord's Prayer cries aloud for comment. 'And forgive us our trespasses, as we forgive them that trespass against us', to which in Matthew 6.15 this verse is added 'But if ye forgive not men their trespasses, neither will your Father forgive your trespasses'. Or as the New

English Bible has it, 'For if you forgive others the wrongs they have done, your heavenly Father will also forgive you; but if you do not forgive others, then the wrongs you have done will not be forgiven by your Father'. What is this? A kind of *quid pro quo*? No, it is a recognition that if our hearts are hardened towards our fellows they will not be in a condition to be able to repent towards God. We are not isolated individuals, we are locked in with the people around us. What they do, perhaps even what they think, affects us; and what we do, and perhaps even think, affects them. It is quite useless therefore to visit the confessional in a state of unforgiving anger on account of some harm done to us, whether we plead the crucifixion or not, God will not forgive us, or to speak more accurately, we will not be able to receive his forgiveness. There is nothing automatic about the crucifixion and God's forgiveness. It is not a transaction over our heads. We have to play our part, not in order to earn forgiveness, no one can do that, but in order to be in fit state to receive it.

I return then to my text from Acts 3.19, 'Repent then and turn to God, so that your sins may be wiped out'. This is what St Peter said to the Jews in Jerusalem smarting with the part they had played in the crucifixion. Repentance was what was asked of them, costly repentance even for what they did in ignorance. Repentance is what opens the door of our hearts so as to be able to receive the forgiveness of our sins God the Father longs to give, cost what it may, even the crucifixion.

16

PREACHING THE HEALING CHRIST

. . . be it known to you all, and to all the people of Israel, that by the name of Jesus Christ of Nazareth, whom you crucified, whom God raised from the dead, by him this man is standing before you well.

ACTS 4.10 (RSV)

I wish we could see him. I wonder what he looked like. Dressed in rags no doubt but with a head held high in spite of the unfamiliar surroundings of the Jerusalem court room. And there opposite him sat Annas the high priest, and Caiaphas and John and Alexander, and all who were of the high priest's family, enough to frighten anyone. But he was not alone, by him stood two apostles, Peter and John, and they were not in the least cowed. He had seen them near Solomon's portico at the Jerusalem Temple where as a helpless cripple he had been deposited daily to beg for alms. They gave him no alms but something far better, health and healing. Peter said 'In the name of Jesus Christ of Nazareth, walk', with a pull of his right hand as Jesus used to do, and the cripple not only stood on his feet and started to walk, but entered the Temple leaping and praising God, as well he might.

1 PREACHING

Now these opening chapters of the book of the Acts of the Apostles describe the early days of the Christian Church which came into being significantly on the day of Pentecost. They give special attention to the message preached of which summaries are provided. Everything turned on the crucifixion and resurrection of Jesus Christ of Nazareth. What had happened was not soft-pedalled, blame was squarely laid and repentance called for but absolutely no revenge and no prophesies of dire consequences to follow. This was the first distinctive mark of the apostolic preaching of the crucifixion as set out in chapter 3 of the book;

and the second distinctive mark was the health and healing ministry which accompanied the preaching. So the crucifixion was for healing, not for hatred, echoing the famous words from the Fourth Servant Song (so called) in Isaiah 53, 'with his stripes we are healed'.

Let me set out what happened. When this nameless and wretched mendicant was seen walking, leaping and praising God in the Temple, someone known to the worshippers even if they had grown accustomed to him squatting there on the floor, a hopeless and helpless cripple from birth, begging, not surprisingly they came running to see. Quite a crowd gathered. And at the centre was the ecstatic cripple clutching hold of his healers. Peter then recognizing the opportunity for testimony preached to them the crucified and risen Christ as the one by whom the cripple now stood upright on his feet.

But not everyone was thrilled. The controllers of the Temple hearing what was going on took alarm. Excited crowds in public places can be dangerous. So together with the chief priests they burst upon the listening people, arrested Peter and John and marched them to the prison for the night, it being already evening. The real cause of their alarm was the story circulating that there were already some five thousand believers in this Jesus whom they had recently crucified and judged to be safely out of the way. Clearly this Jesus movement had to be crushed. They sensed trouble. Next day therefore the two apostles were brought into the court—was it the same place where Jesus had been tried and before the same judges, the notorious Annas and Caiaphas?—and the erstwhile cripple was stood beside them. An enquiry was opened. 'By what power or by what name have such men as you done this?' It was a straight question and it received a straight answer. It was 'by the name of Jesus Christ of Nazareth whom you crucified, whom God raised from the dead that this man stands before you fit and well'. And there he was, head held high, we may guess. The judges were baffled. Here was incontrovertible evidence of healing; the very same as accompanied the preaching of Jesus himself. Apparently this was to accompany the proclamation of the crucified and risen Christ, there was nothing they could do but feebly caution Peter and John to stop preaching altogether in the name of Jesus. But the cured cripple who was over forty years of age was a more powerful sign of the health-giving message of Jesus than any court ruling could ever be.

2 HEALING

The preaching of the Church therefore, the preaching of the crucifixion and of the resurrection, is not to be a mere matter of words. It is to be accompanied by actions. Actions speak louder than words. There have to be words however to explain the actions. The cripple cured by Peter and John was not simply stood in the court room proving incontrovertible evidence of his healing. An explanation was provided and that explanation was Jesus Christ crucified and risen. So there must be preaching and there must be works of compassionate healing in the ministry of the Church. There have been times when the concentration has been on either the one or the other. This will lead to confusion and in the end to the fading out of the Christian Gospel. It is not for nothing that the story of the healing of the cripple so that he could walk, leap and praise God is placed in the very forefront of the early Church's ministry, and not only that, but embedded in the proclamation of the crucified and risen Christ. What the apostles proclaimed was the healing Christ.

I would have you notice that this cured cripple was encountered at random. Peter and John were on their way to the Temple to pray and this wretched man and his pitiable plight caught their attention, pleading for money. They must have passed such cases time and time again, perhaps even this very man himself. What is more he provided no evidence of religious awareness, let alone repentance and faith, he was a hopeless and helpless cripple and had been for forty years. But that he was a man in need was enough. In the name of Jesus Christ of Nazareth he was healed. This openness must ever be the characteristic of the Church's ministry. It must be definite in its preaching, it must preach Christ crucified and risen, but it must be ready to stretch out the hands of healing wherever there is need—and if I may be permitted to use a somewhat rough phrase—with 'no strings attached'. Sometimes the healed man or woman will turn back and praise God for his mercies, sometimes not. When Jesus himself healed ten lepers only one returned to thank him, but he continued with his healing ministry. When the Church carries out its ministry in this way it provides testimony to the love of God which is far broader than the measure of man's mind; and when it does so in the name of Christ crucified the crucifixion itself will cease to be an impenetrable mystery. Let the Church then support its schools, its hospitals, its clinics and its first aid centres whenever there is a need to be met. This is preaching Christ crucified and risen.

Here perhaps it needs to be said that not all ministries are specific healing ministries with the laying-on of hands. Such a ministry is a gift of the Divine Spirit outpoured at Pentecost. It is given to the Church as a whole and some members have it individually. But all members of the Church have not identical gifts. They differ. Some heal, some preach and teach, some administer, but all with a common allegiance to the crucified and risen Lord. The total ministry of the Church where it is faithful and true to its origins and its calling is of the healing Christ in one way or another.

3 QUALITY OF LIFE

I am running into the danger of becoming too technical and too specific in this sermon. What in the main proclaims the Christian Gospel is not schools and colleges, nor captivating preaching nor remarkable ministries of healing but quality of life on the part of ordinary Christian people in all walks of life.

The late Dr Leslie Weatherhead, one time Methodist Minister of the City Temple in London in the 1930s, told this story. It concerned a Turkish officer who raided and looted an Armenian home. He killed the father and mother and gave the daughters to the soldiers, keeping the eldest girl for himself. At last she escaped. She trained as a nurse. Eventually she found herself nursing in a ward of Turkish officers. One night by the light of a lantern she saw the face of this officer. She realized that just to be inattentive, no more, would mean his death that night. Later the doctor said to the officer 'But for this girl's devotion you would be dead'. As he looked to see who it was, he said 'I think we have met before. Why didn't you kill me?' 'I am a follower of him who said, "Love your enemies' " came the reply.

When the preacher in church on Sunday has finished the sermon and the priest has carried the communion vessels back to the vestry and the congregation has dispersed to their various homes to take up on the day following, and all the days after, their routine life, *the way they do it* may be a continuation of that Christian proclamation, possibly to people who never darken the door of a Church building. Their attitude to men and women they dislike and even want to hate, the way they face disappointment, the way they take illness and even crippling losses, without a word spoken can be preaching, Christian preaching of the Christ who 'endured the Cross despising the shame'. Quality of life is the most effective preaching providing incontrovertible evidence of the power of the Gospel, to change people, to change situations and to change even whole communities. It is a healing Gospel, a practical Gospel, and it crosses frontiers. Barriers of race, culture and temperament do not block it off. Christ was crucified and rose again for the healing of us all.

17

GOD'S STRATEGY

God shows his love for us in that while we were yet sinners Christ died for us.

ROMANS 5.8 (RSV)

I would like you to try and imagine yourself going from person to person in a hospital casualty ward. Here is a woman who has slipped on the kitchen floor and broken her leg. She tells you all about it, what she was doing at the time, and how is she to manage the weekend shopping? Here is a young man with an arm swollen up like a balloon, he is a gardener who was cutting the long grass at the edge of a lawn and disturbed a wasps' nest. Here is a boy from school, here a girl from a swimming pool, here is . . . here is . . . On and on you go listening to story after story, how all these injuries happened. And then you follow the doctor into his surgery. He is only marginally interested in what each patient was doing at the time of the accident and how they will manage their life next week, he is concentrating his attention on bone structures, blood samples and temperature charts, all of them matters not fastened upon or understood by patients' minds.

1 THE CRUCIFIXION AND GOD

Now the presentation of the crucifixion in the New Testament has at least a similarity to this situation. In the four gospels the story of the crucifixion is indeed described in some detail and I have been at pains in these sermons to set out what happened. It is not unlike the experience of entering the casualty ward and hearing how the accidents came about. But when we turn to the rest of the New Testament, especially the letters of St Paul, we enter another world. No attempt is made whatsoever to probe into who was actually responsible for the crucifixion whether Jews or Romans, or Pilate, or Herod, or Caiaphas, or Judas

Iscariot. Glaringly, St Paul turns away from all these historical details of what happened and goes researching instead with one instrument of enquiry, coming up with this startling conclusion: God was in the crucifixion. So such texts as the following stand out in his writings: 'God shows his love towards us in that while we were yet sinners Christ died for us' (Romans 5.8); and this: 'God was in Christ reconciling the world to himself' (2 Corinthians 5.19). In a nutshell, the gospels, particularly the first three, present the crucifixion historically, the epistles theologically. It is to the latter now that we turn.

Now I know, of course, that some people, even some Christians, are biased against St Paul. They reckon he distorted the simple story of Jesus and built up in its place a complicated series of theological abstractions. They don't like him. And since it is fashionable nowadays to drag in sex on the flimsiest of excuses they mark him down as having repressive, even warped, ideas about it. This is an entirely wrong position to adopt with regard to St Paul and his place in the New Testament. Leave him out, refuse to read him, block off the mind from wrestling with what he has to say—yes, I agree some wrestling is necessary—but the result will be a poverty-stricken grasp of what the crucifixion is about, especially about God, about ourselves and the relationship between the two. This is the heart of St Paul's presentation. God, not man, was the prime mover in the crucifixion.

This sounds simple enough to say, and in a way it is simple. That is, simple as a key is simple but unlocks doors into places far from simple. So does the basic statement that God, not man, was the prime mover in the crucifixion. As a result we do not look out on Jesus as someone acting on his own; he was not some lonely and courageous Galilean hero who rose from obscurity to champion the cause of humanity, paying the price of losing his life for his faithfulness but in the event altering the course of history. Unaccountable things do happen in the world and this was perhaps the most striking. Nor, to look at the matter religiously, was he a martyr whom God rewarded by raising him from the dead. No, God was *involved* in the crucifixion. I do not mean involved in the sense that he did not come down from heaven to stop such a ghastly event taking place, I mean God was in and behind what happened from start to finish, indeed he was never apart from it. This is how St Paul could write 'God did not spare his own Son but gave him up for us all' (Romans 8.32). Primarily therefore the crucifixion tells us something about God and what is his attitude always to us all. It does not stand simply as an historical event, it proclaims a message, indeed a Gospel, a thing of good news, for all time and for all people everywhere. This is why Paul wrote 'but we preach Christ crucified'. The crucifixion tells us about God.

2 WHERE GOD IS REVEALED

This is disconcerting. I do not mean because the crucifixion was cruel, ugly and repulsive, bringing out the worst in the men who did it, though it was all that and more. I mean it is disconcerting that we should have to go to such a place to see what God is like. It sounds like upside-down thinking, indeed, standing common sense on its head. And if in listening to me now this is your reaction then I have to tell you you are not the first so to respond. The people in Corinth who heard St Paul preach this wrote it off as foolishness. Need we be surprised? They were Greeks with a long tradition of philosophical thinking for which their nation was famous. How could they possibly sit still and hear human wisdom put down as a useless instrument with which to know God? It wasn't as if St Paul was saying human wisdom is imperfect, even faulty, and will in the future rise above its limitations. No, human wisdom never will know God, however competent it may show itself for a thousand other pursuits. All that attempts to know God by a system of abstract reasoning add up to is a record of failure. God can only be known in so far as he reveals himself and this he did supremely in the crucifixion. See my text: 'God shows his love for us in that while we were yet sinners Christ died for us'. God then is revealed in weakness, revealed in the death of Christ. I repeat, this is disconcerting, it sounds like stark intellectual nonsense.

But there was wisdom in the crucifixion, God's wisdom. It shattered the human boasting that mankind without God is quite capable of understanding the world and saving it from chaos. There was also power in the crucifixion, God's power. It is seen in those who commit themselves to the God revealed in the crucifixion. Humble they may be by an ordinary reckoning but they turn out to exhibit strengths of character and achievement, sometimes impressive. So much so that St Paul was able to appeal to the experience of those in Rome who had responded to the Gospel he preached there: 'Therefore, since we are justified by faith, we have peace with God through our Lord Jesus Christ. Through him we have obtained access to this grace in which we stand, and we rejoice in our hope of sharing the glory of God. More than that, we rejoice in our sufferings, knowing that suffering produces endurance, and endurance produces character, and character produces hope, and hope does not disappoint us, because God's love has been poured into our hearts through the Holy Spirit which has been given to us' (Romans 5.1–5). Yes, there is wisdom and there is power in the crucifixion as nowhere else.

3 THE GOD WHO IS REVEALED

What is God like then who is revealed in the crucifixion? He is a God who experiences pain. The world is full of pain, it always has been. There is no birth without pain, no life without pain. The story of mankind is shot through with pain, physical and psychological. None of the vast improvements in living conditions have left pain behind as an unknown thing. To some people this is a convincing argument for the absence of God, the reason for atheism, but the crucifixion cries aloud that God does not sit in isolated majesty above pain and *suffering*. God suffers. He not only suffers, he shares *our suffering*. Christ was not crucified on an isolated exhibition platform but between two angry lawbreakers suffering *with them*, suffering *as they suffered*, all in the staring presence of a gloating public. This is not a revelation of God to be found anywhere but in the crucifixion.

There is more to be said, much more. God suffers with us, yes, but paradoxically he also stands over against us, 'separate from sinners', which is what we are in his sight. Listen to the text again, 'God shows his love for us in that while we were yet sinners Christ died for us'. God is holy, which is what is meant by 'separate from sinners', but he does not simply demand that we acknowledge his holiness, he died *for us* painfully who come nowhere near attaining it. But what do the words mean, 'He died *for us*'? Did he die in our place? That is to say, we are guilty sinners but Christ the sinless One is our substitute before the judgement throne of God? The crucifixion has been preached with this interpretation. Or do the words 'He died *for us*' mean he was faithful unto death as our representative accomplishing a life of perfect sacrifice to which we could not possibly attain? We may recoil from either or both of these interpretations but we ought to remember that they, and others like them also far from perfect, have assisted men and women to receive the peace of God offered in the crucifixion. All interpretations of the crucifixion are only partial of what remains as a mystery, the mystery of the Divine Presence and operation for mankind.

The wise course is to rest our souls in what is crystal clear, God is a God of grace, sovereign grace. He gave himself for us the undeserving. This is what grace is, God's free favour for the undeserving. It proceeds from love, not a sentimental attitude, but costly action. So our text again from Romans 5.8: 'God shows his love for us in that while we were yet sinners Christ died for us'. This is the Gospel. This is the good news of the crucifixion proclaimed by St Paul and preached by the Church in the ministry of word and sacrament. It calls for our acceptance.

18

THE CRUCIFIXION—RESURRECTION EVENT

If Christ has not been raised, your faith is futile and you are still in your sins.

1 CORINTHIANS 15.17 (RSV)

I begin this sermon with a story, a true one, of an ultra-Protestant vicar who removed the brass ornamental cross from the shelf behind the Communion table in his church and replaced it with a white card bearing the words 'Christ is risen'. It was a true proclamation. Christ *is* risen. My complaint, however, is that the resurrection does not do away with the crucifixion. They belong together as God's double mighty act for our salvation. Perhaps he should have left the cross where it was and placed his card there as well, that is if he didn't mind how inartistic the combination looked. And would not a plain cross, and not a crucifix, have met his point? Be that as it may, the poor man has gone to heaven now and perhaps sees things differently. In any case I only tell the story to reinforce the point which is the subject of this sermon, the crucifixion and the resurrection belong together as one comprehensive action. The acclamation in Rite A of the ASB Communion has got it right:

> Christ has died
> Christ is risen
> Christ will come again.

1 THE UGLY CRUCIFIX

There is a little incident in one of W.B. Yeats's stories which has stuck in my mind. A young Irish girl coming into a room had her eyes caught by a crucifix on the wall, a familiar object in Roman Catholic homes in Ireland. Pointing to it, she screamed 'Take that ugly thing away!' The family was shocked.

But a crucifix is ugly. The crucifixion was ugly. Everything about it was ugly. The minds that could invent such a ghastly instrument of torture and the minds that could order it to be used. The crucifixion shows up the worst in human nature. But what is even more repulsive is the recognition that civilization, so called, has not abandoned torture as an instrument of political policy throughout the world. To this very day the horror continues. It is on this account that a cross is, in many minds, a proper symbol, the crucifixion is not outmoded. Life is little short of a crucifixion for too many people.

No doubt this sounds like an overstatement. Certainly in the prosperous countries of the northern hemisphere people derive a great deal of pleasure, if not fun, out of life, but the fun is fleeting and fails to produce a state of happiness. The index is the thousands upon thousands of people who only keep going with the deceitful aid of drugs and excessive alcohol. The real trouble is that life seems meaningless, and in this slough of despond the buoyancy of hopes and aspirations become lost. So the melancholy cross in the midst of our prosperity reflects the modern moods of disillusionment. It is here that we touch upon the reason why contemporary man has no ears for the preaching of the resurrection, life isn't like that; but the cross, the crucifixion, is what he knows in experience. There are very few happy endings and if that is what Easter Day following Good Friday stands for, better rub it out. Bluntly speaking, it is not true to life, whereas the crucifixion is.

2 THE RESURRECTION COMPLETES THE CRUCIFIXION

Now the Christian Church does not give prominence to the crucifixion because it acts as a reflection of human depression about life in general. Quite the reverse. It carries a liberating message, liberation from the bondage of sin both cosmic and personal. The heart of the Christian proclamation is forgiveness and this is brought about by the crucifixion and what God in Christ did for us there. We cannot however sit back on the assumption that nothing more is to be said, nothing more done, for a transaction has accomplished all. It is true there needs to be no more divine offering for sin as the epistle to the Hebrews, chapter 10 is at pains to point out but the crucifixion does not stand on its own, what God did there was completed in the resurrection on Easter Day. St Paul is categorical on this. He who wrote in 1 Corinthians 15.3, 'For I delivered to you as of first importance what I also received, that Christ died for our sins in accordance with the scriptures', also wrote, fourteen verses later, 'If Christ has not been raised, your faith is futile and you are still in your sins'. Strong words these! 'Your faith is futile.' They mean that what was accomplished in the crucifixion only becomes operative in us because of the resurrection. It is the resurrection that calls forth faith, faith in the crucifixion as God's purposeful act and faith in God as a God of love and of power hidden under a veil of weakness.

It is just here that the importance of telling the Good Friday and Easter Day story as set out in the gospels becomes evident. As we read of the women on the road to the cross weeping, as we visualize the disciples skulking back in their lodgings in Jerusalem because of what had taken place at Golgotha, as we think of the depths of despair they plumbed because they had hoped Jesus might be the Messiah and who could not therefore die but was now actually dead and buried, we can grasp how the resurrection changed their thought of the crucifixion dramatically. A thrill shook the hearts and minds of every follower of Jesus who had continued with him up to the shattering spectacle of that ugly cross, and brought them to life. So the resurrection made the crucifixion effective. Until the resurrection took place the crucifixion was ineffective as a spiritual power, it stood there as an embarrassing puzzle.

What this means is that the Church must emphasize the crucifixion and the resurrection together. If all the weight is given to the former there will result a discipleship of gloom; sin and death will colour even the form of worship. There is perhaps a tendency towards this in the Book of Common Prayer. If on the other hand the themes of suffering and defeat are suppressed there will appear a kind of triumphalism which will not square with the mixed bag of experiences which life serves up to us. Balance is perhaps the most necessary requirement in the right ordering of Christian worship, and one the most difficult to achieve.

3 THE CRUCIFIXION IS TO BE PREACHED

And now a third consideration. This collection of sermons carries the title *Preaching on the Crucifixion*. It is a startling title, at first puzzling, if not offensive, just as if anyone would contemplate proclaiming, or indeed publicizing at all, least of all in Christian worship, such a horrible event. But the resurrection is what has caused it to be preached. It has caused the crucifixion to speak to us, tell us somthing vital for the whole world. And so the crucifixion and the resurrection together have evoked the ministry of preaching. It was immediately after the crucifixion on Good Friday, and the resurrection on Easter Day, that St Peter in particular and the apostles in general stood up to preach, not before, and all under the influence of the power of Divine spirit outpoured.

The crucifixion then is to be preached. And wherever there is Christian preaching it should be in the light of Christ crucified, indeed the whole teaching ministry of the pulpit should be illumined by it. There is a custom in many churches to position a crucifix on the wall close to the pulpit. Well and good, but let the preaching be in alignment with it and not so distant that the hearers could be forgiven for wondering if ever the crucifixion took place or had any relevance to people today. As the Holy Communion is stamped with Christ's death, 'As often as you eat this bread and drink this cup you proclaim the Lord's death till he comes', so ought the preaching. The Christian ministry operates in worship through word and sacrament the basis for which is the crucifixion-resurrection event. From this the Church must not stray. It is its lifeline.

None of all this of course makes any sense apart from the identity of Jesus as the Son of God. It is because of who Jesus was that the Crucifixion–resurrection event is preached. The absolutely essential basis is the Incarnation, God become man and dwelling among us. It is because of this that there is a gospel in the crucifixion proclaiming the forgiveness of sins. It is because of this that the resurrection brings the promise of eternal life to us, and the grave loses its sting. Incarnation, crucifixion, resurrection, the forgiveness of sins and the life eternal interlock. So the words of the Nicene Creed we recite in the Service of Holy Communion; 'I believe in one Lord Jesus Christ, the only begotten Son of God . . . Who for us men and for our salvation . . . was incarnate by the Holy Ghost of the Virgin Mary, and was made man, And was crucified also for us under Pontius Pilate. . . . And the third day he rose again according to the Scriptures . . . I acknowledge one Baptism for the remission of sins, And I look for the Resurrection of the dead, And the life of the world to come.' Let me repeat then the essential basis of our faith, under the heading of three key words—incarnation, crucifixion, resurrection. This is where we have to start and on which we must never lose our hold. And it is my firm conviction that this hold will not be realized unless the stories of the incarnation, crucifixion and resurrection are vividly told and retold. Preachers must be good story-tellers. I cannot help wondering if what are called the Passion narratives in the four gospels are there because these were the stories told in the early Church service of worship, stimulating the minds of those present to grasp what was going on.

I come back to my text, 'If Christ has not been raised, your faith is futile'. Please God our faith in this congregation will not be futile. It will not be if we keep hold of the crucifixion and resurrection of Christ as of eternal significance because he was the incarnate Son of God.

19

HOLY COMMUNION

For as often as you eat this bread and drink the cup, you proclaim the Lord's death until he comes.

1 CORINTHIANS 11.26 (RSV)

Forgive me if I repeat telling you of a tiny experience I had some years ago. On entering what on any reckoning would have to be counted a Low church my attention was caught by a white card leaning against the wall behind the Holy Table where I might have expected, if not a crucifix, certainly a cross. Instead there was this card bearing in bold black lettering the words 'Christ is risen'. When I made enquiries how this came to be I was told the vicar had taken the cross away which used to stand there, replacing it with this card. Now I would not have been shocked to see no ornamental cross in that place, or perhaps a vase of flowers. I knew how some forms of Protestantism react against whatever seems even remotely connected with Catholicism, but to say in effect, as this card implied, that the resurrection has done away with the cross is to stand the New Testament on its head and to rub out the gospel. The crucifixion is the place where God acted for us. No, certainly Christ is not dead. He is risen. He is alive. Were this not so, the crucifixion would be seen as little more than a horrible historical event. But it stands till the end of time as the way for mankind to be in communion with God. This is my subject for this sermon pinpointed in the text from 1 Corinthians 11.26, 'For as often as you eat this bread and drink the cup, you proclaim the Lord's death until he comes'. And for fear lest you should think I have spoken unfairly about Low Church let me add that I knew another Low church where the words of the text were artistically picked out in large gold lettering above the reredos although there was no cross on the table. The crucifixion was firmly and properly connected with the Holy Communion.

1 THE LAST SUPPER

It is the Lord's Supper, the Holy Communion, the Eucharist, the Mass, call it what you will, to which I invite your attention. There are four accounts of its institution in the New Testament, three in the first three gospels and one, the earliest to be written, in St Paul's letter to the Christians in Corinth from which my text is taken. All four accounts are overshadowed by the crucifixion. They all begin 'who in the same night in which he was betrayed'. And so the words are repeated at every celebration of the Holy Communion however simple, however elaborate. Judas Iscariot always stands in the shadows. Communicants are never to forget when this sacrament was instituted and how it was Jesus came to be crucified. The connection between the Eucharist and the crucifixion is thus fixed for all time. 'For as often as you eat this bread and drink the cup, you proclaim the Lord's death until he comes.'

Let me remind you of what happened.

As far as the apostles were concerned, the institution of the Holy Communion was unexpected. It took place in the course of a meal of which Jesus was the host and of which even the location was kept secret till the last moment. Tension was present from the outset. The apostles fell to arguing about seniority, perhaps sparked off by the seating (reclining) arrangements. Then Jesus divested himself of his outer garments, tied a towel around his waist, poured water into a basin and insisted on washing everyone's feet. They did not like it. Worse was to come. Jesus announced that this would be their last meal together. And as if this were not crushing enough, that one of them would betray him to the very men who wanted to kill him. Did they at this point feel for the means to defend him? There were two swords in the room and strong men able to overpower a traitor if they knew who it could be. But they did not know; not even when Jesus dipped a piece of bread in the dish and gave it to Judas. This is what a host did who wanted to honour especially one at the table. They did not know it was the last chance for Judas to break with his nefarious intention. They only saw him rise up from the table, move over to the door, open it and pass out into the night. Were the thirty pieces of silver the priests had given him to betray Jesus tucked into his girdle? Did he spit out on the stairs the bread Jesus had given him? We do not know. All we know is that he hurried to the priests to tell them that Jesus was in a certain upper room in the city and could be apprehended safely. Meanwhile the meal went on.

'As they were eating' (I am quoting from Mark 14, verses 22–24) 'he

91

took bread, and blessed, and broke it, and gave it to them, and said, "Take; this is my body." And he took a cup, and when he had given thanks he gave it to them, and they all drank of it. And he said to them, "This is my blood of the covenant, which is poured out for many." ' After further discourse, a hymn was sung. Then they all made their way to the garden of Gethsemane where Judas, at the head of a crowd with swords and clubs come from the chief priests, scribes and elders, identified Jesus for them with a kiss and the word 'Master'. So he was arrested.

All this is the background of the institution of the Holy Communion summarized vividly in the words repeated at every celebration: 'who in the same night that he was betrayed took bread; and, when he had given thanks, he brake it, and gave it to his disciples, saying, Take, eat; this is my body which is given for you: Do this in remembrance of me.' What he gave the apostles reclining at table was *broken* bread. It was his broken body they received, the body to be crucified in a matter of hours. The Holy Communion and the crucifixion are inextricably tied together. The Holy Communion interprets the crucifixion. The crucifixion interprets the Holy Communion.

2 INTERPRETATION

We turn now to consider this double-sided interpretation. First of all, to ask how the Holy Communion interprets the crucifixion. It does so because in the Holy Communion we *receive*. The broken bread and the poured-out wine are not placed on the Holy Table as exhibits but as the means of giving and receiving. So the crucifixion does not stand in order to present a grim spectacle for all time but so that we can receive what we need for all time and eternity. Indeed it is impossible to resist the conclusion that Jesus instituted the Holy Communion when he did and the way he did, that is, by an action to be repeated and not only by words, as the means by which the meaning of the crucifixion could be grasped by ordinary people. Something is given there and something to be received, and for all time.

This can be expressed another way by saying that the giving and receiving make for communion. It is after all at meals and over meals that fellowship is built up in everyday life. The Holy Communion therefore is the divinely appointed way for human fellowship with God to be experienced. I was going to say 'enjoyed', and why not! Can we not see then in the light of the Holy Communion how the crucifixion took place so that we may have fellowship with God, free access to the Divine Presence, all barriers done away? The cross is the ground of our confidence, no, more, even of joy, the proper reaction to which is thanksgiving. No wonder the Holy Communion is also called the Eucharist, the Greek word for 'giving thanks' taken from 1 Corinthians 11.24.

A third way in which the Holy Communion interprets or throws light on the crucifixion comes when we note how the Holy Communion is, and always has been, at the centre of Christian worship. It is there that our spiritual aspirations become focused and where we most powerfully realize them. So it is with the crucifixion. Indeed if we have not come face to face personally with it we have not entered into the Christian faith. It stands by the front door. There is no back entrance, no side door, no way around it.

I have tried to show how the Eucharist interprets the crucifixion, but what of the converse? Does the crucifixion interpret or throw light on the Eucharist? Yes, it does. The crucifixion is a mystery in the sense that it is difficult to understand how God was really present, yet he was. With it in mind St Paul wrote 'God was in Christ reconciling the world to himself'.

So the real presence of God in the Eucharist is a mystery. He is there, there by his choice, we do not make his presence by our faith. And he is present for our sakes, actively present.

And now this. The crucifixion was manifestly a sacrifice, Christ's sacrifice. The Holy Communion cannot escape the principle of sacrifice. It is embedded at the heart of the service. And the Christian life cannot be in the absence of sacrifice. Self-centredness has to go, a painful, almost unnatural renunciation, almost a kind of crucifixion. Not surprisingly to live as a Christian is sometimes called the Way of the Cross.

And thirdly, the crucifixion is never superseded, not even by the resurrection, the miracle which of course transforms our whole outlook. Nor can the Eucharist be superseded. We can never suggest that in future we worship God another way. The Holy Communion stands for all time as our place of meeting with God.

3 PREACHING

This sermon has already been lengthy, repeating some of what I have said before. So I must finish briefly. Lest however we have lost sight of the text at the outset, I must return to it. 1 Corinthians 11.26: 'For as often as you eat this bread and drink the cup, you proclaim the Lord's death until he comes'. The striking point here is that apparently all communicants are preachers, however often they come, however rarely, and whether in AD 100 or AD 2000, or AD 20,000 if that date is reached. Always and everywhere when communicants receive the broken bread and drink from the cup they are proclaiming (the same word is used for preaching) the Lord's death, the crucifixion. They are showing (see Authorized Version at 1 Corinthians 11.26) that it is not a mere historical event but a place to which to come now and for ever. So all communicants are preachers, preachers of the cross of Christ. There have been times, and they are not altogether past, when some Christians have tried to set preaching over against the Holy Communion and the Holy Communion over against preaching. This is wrong. They belong together; there must be preaching and there must be the Holy Communion, for as I have tried to show they interpret each other.

So do not denigrate your pulpit in your Church and do not underrate the sacrament of the Lord's Supper, and if you have an ornamental cross please do not ever think of replacing it with a white card or anything else!

20

WINDOWS ON THE CRUCIFIXION

God was in Christ reconciling the world to himself.

2 CORINTHIANS 5.19 (RSV)

I begin my sermon today by recounting what was told me about a young woman, perhaps in her late twenties, sitting on a bench at one of London's great railway stations during the 'rush hour'. Her train was late and would not be arriving for twenty minutes or more. She was educated, well-dressed and intelligent. Moreover she had had a strict religious upbringing which on occasions weighed heavily upon her, and as she sat on the hard bench watching the crowds hurrying past this turned out to be one of those occasions. She couldn't believe that all these people were earmarked for hell when they died because they had not decided for Christ crucified in the way required of her in the sect to which she and her whole family belonged. It made God seem so cruel, not to say unreasonable. Better be an atheist, better recognize no God at all, than a Being like this. And what about the crucifixion? It took place so long ago. What difference can it make to people now especially if they rarely even give it a thought?

I have often wondered what happened to this woman and I have no idea, but I could wish that I had had the opportunity to try and lead her into a broader yet positive interpretation of the Christian faith especially with regard to the crucifixion, a faith in which there is liberty to believe in the breadth of God's love and the vastness of what Christ accomplished for the whole world at Golgotha. It is this that I have in mind preaching this sermon.

1 THE SIN OF THE WORLD

I have been saying that God was in the crucifixion and that Christ was not acting there *on his own*. I have been saying that God shows his love for us 'in that while we were yet sinners Christ died for us'. Yes, you say, but

95

what does the crucifixion in practice *do for us*? Does it move us, when it is brought home to us how Christ suffered, to live more sacrificial lives ourselves and be willing to put ourselves out for others, and so make the world a better place? In other words, does the crucifixion operate psychologically? Or is it that because of the crucifixion, which was God's act, our standing before the moral law is now altered, in other words a change has come about irrespective of our response to it? So were all the people hurrying along the station platform in London, virtuously oblivious of the crucifixion, nevertheless affected by it? Does it operate, so to speak, over our heads?

Before we attempt to answer this question we have to take the matter of sin seriously, and that is not easily done in the modern climate of secular thinking. The text however that I have been emphasizing does just this. 'God shows his love for us in that *while we were yet sinners* Christ died for us.' It takes for granted that we are sinners, almost as if no one could possibly be so foolish as to deny the fact. And we nod our heads as if to admit that . . . well yes, even in this congregation we, all of us, have strayed now and again from the 'straight and narrow', not that we have lost much sleep over our faults and failings. Perhaps, however, these minor discrepancies are not in mind, but only the outrageous acts of violence and cruelty that have besmirched the notorious tyrants from which millions of people have suffered horribly in this century. The truth is both are in mind, the little deeds which shame us when we think about what we have done and the massive evil deeds perpetrated by people who from time to time receive coverage in the press. Sin is sin whatever its proportions. There is however something beyond little sinful acts and big sinful acts committed by individuals, there is what may be called cosmic sin, sometimes called 'original sin'. Somehow the world is 'out of joint', human nature is basically flawed and no political, social or economic action can put it to rights. It is a task for which progress in the arts and sciences for all their undoubted contribution to the betterment of life is finally inadequate. It is this that makes the story of mankind depressing in spite of the occasional glorious interludes. No, men and women are not bad through and through, we are made 'in the image of God'. And there is beauty and breathtaking wonder in the universe thrilling us the more we come to learn of them. Always, however, widespread evil, often in subtle forms, has to be reckoned with, and the shadow of death. We cannot escape either, and if God provides no escape there is none. This is the context in which we have to see the crucifixion if we are not simply to list it as one more cruel deed in the long history of cruel deeds that men and women have suffered since the world began. The crucifixion was different. It was different because God was in it, and because it concerned the sin of the world, the great cosmic and chronic disorientation from which in greater or less degree we all suffer.

2 WINDOWS NOT THEORIES

If this were a lecture and not a sermon I could at this point list some of the theories that are advanced to explain how the crucifixion deals with the sin of the world and the sins of individuals; and maybe I ought at least to touch on them lest you count my whole handling of this vast subject superficial.

Broadly speaking the various interpretations or theories of the atonement, as technically they are known, have been and are formed in the light of the the thinking of the day in which they are propounded. One of the earliest, arising out of feudalism, understood the crucifixion in legal categories. God is the judge. We are the sinners in the dock. The moral law cannot be flouted. Transgression must be punished, but God is a God of love. The crucifixion however provided the way out of this divine/human dilemma. God sent his only Son, the sinless One, to suffer the punishment for sin *in our place*, the innocent for the guilty. So the requirement of the moral law was satisfied. So for our sakes this transaction was effected.

Not surprisingly this interpretation was rejected by many as immoral—the innocent being punished for the guilty; it was unjust. It also seemed to be saying that God rather than men and women was changed by the crucifixion. And so instead the crucifixion came to be seen as a a *demonstration* of God's love showing the extent to which that love was willing to go for our sakes, and thus inspiring a corresponding sacrificial love from us in return. Here, in this theory, is nothing mechanical, nothing of a transaction. If the satisfaction theory is an objective explanation of the atonement this is a subjective one. It is a psychological understanding and gained popularity in the liberal outlook on religion characteristic of the nineteenth and twentieth centuries.

A third interpretation sees the crucifixion in the context of the age-long struggle between good and evil in the world. The crucifixion was the point at which it reached its climax and where good triumphed. This was God's work and by it the world was reconciled to God. Perhaps this picture of the crucifixion as a place of conflict is easier for us moderns to appreciate and certainly the word 'reconciliation' connected with it because it is often on our lips in connexion with disputes between rival groups and in families. We understand reconciliation. It helps us to understand the crucifixion.

A protest against all these theories comes today especially from what is called 'feminist theology'. All the foregoing theories, propounded in the main by men, rely almost exclusively on reason to the neglect of feeling, and on that account are grossly one-sided and therefore incomplete and inadequate. Some women therefore see the pain of the crucifixion in terms of the pain of childbirth. New life, new being indeed, is brought about by the agony of the crucifixion and is made evident by the resurrection which followed. Thus Good Friday and Easter Day are held together as intrinsic parts of God's great act of love on behalf of us all.

Four possible explanations then, of what the crucifixion effected. The temptation is to opt for one and reject the others. This is wrong. The Godhead is a profound mystery and so is his work in the crucifixion. We see something, of course we see something, otherwise it would be meaningless. Any explanation, however, we may have can be no more than *one window* through which, possibly, we catch a glimpse, maybe only for a time, of what God was doing for us at Golgotha. Yet we must trust the little we see for by means of it we shall be brought into the presence of God, and that is satisfaction enough.

3 COMPREHENSIVE SALVATION

I come back to the young woman sitting on a bench at a great London railway terminus puzzled by the incongruity of a God of love and the idea that all these hurrying passengers, passing her by, were destined for perdition if they had no personal knowledge of a conversion experience, which she had been brought up to believe was essential for salvation. What a pity no one was sitting beside her to remind her of my text for this sermon, 'God was in Christ reconciling *the world* to himself', not simply those who believe or even know about him. And verses such as 'As in Adam all die even so in Christ shall *all* be made alive'. The crucifixion–resurrection of Christ was universal in its scope. This means that the Gospel of his death and resurrection is not preached in order that those who respond to it may receive salvation but in order to let us know what was accomplished for us all that first Good Friday and Easter Day. The preaching of this Gospel is liberating. This is the word of the cross. See it this way and we shall not fall into the error of imagining that evangelism is no longer necessary.

Perhaps I may make the point with an illustration. Here is a boy caught up in war in the Far East, exiled from his country, from his home and all members of his family. He gets taken into a huge refugee camp, an anonymous lone child. He knows no one. After some months to his astonishment he is taken away and set on a ship bound for North America. A bright and intelligent boy, he is entered for a school and does well. Later on he succeeds in a well-paid job and ought to be contented, and so he is in a way, but one question will never let him rest. Who is he? Who were his parents and how did he come to be placed on that ship bound for freedom in the United States? Now my question. If someone knew the answer to the riddle in this boy's life would it be right to withhold the knowledge from the now grown-up young man? Would it not contribute to his wellbeing to be told of his benefactor and so gain an identity? The answer is obvious. So it is right to tell people, as they are able to hear it, what God in Christ has done for us all so that they might rise to the stature which God intended. Universalism or what has been achieved for every man and woman in the crucifixion and resurrection does not cancel out the preaching of the Gospel, it reinforces it. I wish the young woman on the station could have believed this.

21

TWO OTHER CRUCIFIXIONS

*There were two others with him, criminals who were being led away to
execution; and when they reached the place called The Skull, they
crucified him there, and the criminals with him, one on his right and
the other on his left.*

LUKE 23.32, 33

If you were a preacher—I fancy I can overhear you saying to yourself,
'God forbid!' Very well, but if you were, and if furthermore you had a
better understanding than that the essence of preaching is pompously to
tell people 'where they get off', whereas of course it is nothing of the
kind, you would have to make up your mind, as I have had to make up
my mind, not least in today's sermon, about two questions. Am I going
to avoid all subjects concerning which there may be more than one point
of view? And secondly, am I going to be sufficiently open and honest to
admit that concerning some matters I simply do not know the answers?
On these I remain an agnostic though a reverent one, not a scoffing
agnostic, for such a person is stupidly arrogant. There may well come a
time when we know what we at present do not know. Till then it is wise
to leave some problems, as it were, in the pending file. There are of
course things which every preacher must believe with all his heart or he
has no place in any Christian pulpit at all; first and foremost is the fact of
Christ, incarnate, crucified and risen. Preaching is essentially proclaiming Christ and no preaching ministry which does not so proclaim Christ
is preaching at all as understood by the New Testament. Questions however arise and they are not all easy to answer.

Here is one question. Does the self-sacrifice of Christ in the crucifixion reconcile us all to God, or only those who have heard the Christian Gospel and responded in repentance and faith? And if the former,
why trouble to preach the Gospel? And if the latter, is it fair? For many
people, perhaps by far the great majority, have never even heard of
Christ let alone had the chance to respond to him. Those of us who have
been brought up with the Book of Common Prayer may recall the

sentence in the Consecration Prayer in the Holy Communion, 'who made there (by his one oblation of himself once offered) a full, perfect, and sufficient sacrifice, oblation, and satisfaction, for the sins of the whole world; . . .'. And those with a fair knowledge of the New Testament may remember the text 'God was in Christ reconciling the world to himself, no longer holding men's misdeeds against them' (2 Corinthians 5.19). The question then is of a selective salvation or a general salvation. This is what I shall attempt to handle in this sermon, and I shall do so on the basis of the story of the two other crucifixions that took place when Jesus hung on the central cross on Good Friday at the place that was called 'The Skull'.

1 THE CRIMINAL WHO REPENTED

We begin with the crucifixion procession because that is what took place, if we can disabuse ourselves of anything like dignity in connection with it. Jesus was indeed in a procession, he was not alone on the way to the crucifixion site. There were two other men being marched along or prodded along with him, each carrying a board inscribed with his crime. Was it bandit, robber, instigator of revolt? Anyway all could read it. No doubt the onlookers hurled insults in varying degrees of vulgarity. Then came Jesus not carrying his cross like the other two but followed by a man whom the execution squad had seized in the crowd and on whose shoulders they put it. Both these condemned criminals taunted Jesus, like many in the crowd, for being God's chosen One but unable to save himself. Both were Christ-mockers. Then all three were nailed up on the crosses, Jesus in between the other two. A strange conversation is reported to have followed. It is to this we turn our attention.

Apparently one of the two criminals suddenly changed his mind. Why he did so we have no idea. But listening to the taunt of his fellow victim, 'Are not you the Messiah? Save yourself and us', and without addressing Jesus directly, he answered the man sharply: 'Have you no fear of God? You are under the same sentence as he. For us it is plain justice; we are paying the price of our misdeeds, but this man has done nothing wrong.' This, of course, is nothing more nor less than repentance, or change of mind. This criminal, from seeing Christ as an object of ribaldry, suddenly saw him as one to whom to make his last appeal. We may ask what made this one change his mind and not the other. Both were in the same condemnation. Both had the same Christ beside them. Both presumably had heard the same words on Jesus' lips: 'Father, forgive them for they know not what they do'. One repented, only one. Why not the other? We do not know. So it always has been and still is. One responds to the Gospel, the other does not.

And then for the first time the repentant criminal addressed Jesus directly, 'Jesus, remember me when you come to your throne'. This is remarkable. It means that this caught, condemned and crucified criminal saw that Jesus although now impaled on a cross was not being defeated in his kingdom but was actually coming into it. It means that he saw through the horror of the crucifixion to the glory of his crown. It means that he saw stretching out before him an eternity to come and gathering up all his fast diminishing strength he made his appeal to him whom he recognized as its King. 'Jesus, remember me when you come to your throne.'

We should note he did not ask to be let off the penalty of his wrongdoing. He knew he was shortly to die but he made his appeal to him whom he recognized to be the supreme judge not to forget him. In the light of this it is impossible to confuse forgiveness with remission of the price of sin. This man had broken the law and now the law had broken him. And if we break God's laws whether of health or morality we shall pay for our misdeeds, not least in impaired health. But if we repent and turn, whatever our misdeeds, we shall not be cast out and forgotten. 'Jesus remember me' cried the criminal and there came back an assurance greater than he either asked or expected, Jesus answered 'I tell you this: today you shall be with me in Paradise'. He asked to be remembered at some distant time. He was promised Paradise before the day was out.

2 THE OTHER CRIMINAL

We turn now to the other criminal, the one who did not repent, the one who addressed nothing to Christ except taunts and insults and to whom Christ said nothing. The penitent was promised Paradise, what was the destiny of the impenitent? Or to broaden the question, what is the destiny of the millions of people in the world who have never heard and never responded in faith to Christ crucified, by far the greater majority? These two other crucifixions on Skull Hill provoke two differing reactions, one of profound thankfulness for the Gospel of God's grace for sinners, the other a huge and disturbing question mark not simply about the fate of the impenitent criminal cursing and rebellious till his final breath but whether or not the sacrifice of Christ on the central cross *in any way* covers him and the millions and millions of people, whom he represents, lacking even the fleeting contact with Christ that he experienced. Nor is this all. The stark question disturbingly posed by the two other crucifixions is about the crucifixion of Jesus. Was it really for the whole world or only for a tiny minority? Is there a general salvation, or only a selective salvation?

Perhaps this is a harder question for us today than at the time of the crucifixion and the decades, even centuries, that immediately followed it. The world was conceived as a much smaller place then, but now there is brought home to us the vastness of the universe and the teeming population of this one planet. It might just be possible in the close-knit Roman empire with its network of communications to believe that all would hear of Christ and his crucifixion and be able to make a response, I said 'just possible' though that is straining the likelihood, but to make this suggestion in the light of our modern knowledge of the size of the world's far-flung population is preposterous. We have to face the fact that the crucifixion of Christ was a local event in a far-off age. And so there is forced on us the disturbing question how this can possibly have an effect on us today.

3 WHO WAS ON THE CENTRAL CROSS?

It can, of course, have some effect if we are content to see Jesus as a teacher who, although living in a bygone age, spoke such sublime, even timeless truths that they have relevance to every age, even ours. After all Jesus is not the only teacher of antiquity whose words are still studied and applied to contemporary life. But do the titles 'teacher', 'healer', 'prophet' and such like adequately describe him? I am bound to say that I do not think we shall even approach an understanding of the significance of the crucifixion unless we have come round to the Church's conviction about Jesus that he was *God incarnate*. Well may we ask how the death of this one man in AD 29 in Judaea could have any effect except on the tiniest minority of mankind. But suppose in him human nature itself has been taken up, that is the human nature of everyone who is human, which of course includes both the criminals who were crucified, one on each side of him, then the crucifixion of Christ and his resurrection has universal consequences. Forgive me if I relapse into theological language for a moment. I can do no other. Jesus was/is the Word of God, God made visible, God the Creator made visible, even tangible, the source and sustainer of *all life throughout all time*. It was he who was crucified on that central cross. What he achieved there cannot therefore be restricted to human response in order to operate, however important that response may be for the individual or community that makes it. In the crucifixion *God the Creator* was in Christ reconciling *his* world to himself. He is the universal Saviour, *Salvator Mundi*. We shall never appreciate this length, breadth, depth and height until we are prepared to see the atonement in connexion with the incarnation.

Yes, questions arise. Someone wishes to say, why bother then with preaching the gospel if salvation is universal anyway? Because whatever may be the value of an inheritance it will not profit unless its existence and worth are made known. Maybe to reject the inheritance God in Christ has opened up through the crucifixion and resurrection, and so be outside it, *is possible*. I don't know, but I believe it is open to all. The words in the Consecration Prayer have expressed this truth forcefully: 'Who made there (by his one oblation of himself once offered) a full, perfect, and sufficient sacrifice, oblation, and satisfaction, for the sins of the *whole world*'. Some of us may have difficulty with this concept of 'satisfaction' but the truth of a universal atonement is what it wishes to safeguard.

I return to the text from Luke 23.32, 33: 'There were two others with him, criminals who were being led away to execution; and when they reached the place called The Skull they crucified him there, and the criminals with him, one on his right and the other on his left'. In our right and proper concentration of attention on the central victim, do not forget the two other crucifixions. He hung there *for both of them* and for all whom they represent, for he was God incarnate, God the Creator incarnate.

22

NO OTHER GLORY

But far be it from me to glory except in the cross of our Lord Jesus Christ, by which the world has been crucified to me, and I to the world.

GALATIANS 6.14 (RSV)

I wonder what you would think if I said, or indeed if any other preacher said, that the Christian life is hard. Would you say to yourself: Yes it certainly is; out in the world today, being a Christian is like trying to swim against the tide. And it requires a good deal of courage, specially on the part of the young, to endure the rude remarks so often made about someone dubbed 'religious', and treated as if he/she were a simpleton. And the Christian way of life certainly is hard. It never has been easy. To go straight, to keep clean hands and a clean mind requires considerable effort, but I bring to your notice another kind of hardship, specially for good people and religious people. This is to abandon the natural habit of grounding our acceptance by God in our own charitable performance in life. There is a whole book about this in the New Testament called the epistle to the Galatians, the theme of which is summed up in St Paul's words which constitute my text, 'But far be it from me to glory except in the cross of our Lord Jesus Christ, by which the world has been crucified to me, and I to the world'.

1 THE USELESSNESS OF SELF-COMMENDATION

And you say to me, 'O well, that is St Paul, he is always a bit gloomy, theoretical and abstract'; but did not Jesus himself make the same point, only he put it in story form? Listen: 'Two men went into the Temple to pray, one a Pharisee, the other a tax collector. The Pharisee stood and prayed thus with himself, "God I thank thee that I am not like other men, extortioners, unjust, adulterers, or even like this tax collector. I fast twice a week, I give tithes of all that I get." But the tax collector, standing far off, would not even lift up his eyes to heaven, but beat his breast, saying, "God, be merciful to me a sinner!" I tell you, this man went down to his house justified rather than the other; for everyone who exalts himself will be humbled, but he who humbles himself will be exalted.'

So wasn't St Paul in line with Christ when he wrote 'But far be it from me to glory except in the cross of our Lord Jesus Christ, by which the world has been crucified to me, and I to the world'? In other words, everything is out when it comes to the matter of our justification before God, nothing we have done, said, promised or not done, counts at all in this matter—only one thing, the crucifixion of Christ by means of which the barriers between ourselves and acceptance by God have been swept away. As St Paul wrote in another letter, this time to the Corinthians (2 Corinthians 5.19): 'God was in Christ, reconciling the world unto himself, not counting their trespasses against them'. It is because of the cross of Christ we can stand in God's presence, and for no other reason at all.

2 THE WAY OF THE CROSS

Now if it is too much to claim that what I have just said about our total inability to commend ourselves to God is humiliating, it certainly 'cuts us down to size'. We are on the ground floor and we cannot reach up to God. He must reach down to us and he did it in the crucifixion. But there is more to be said, we cannot know the *nature of God* apart from the crucifixion, we think we can. We argue from theoretical first principles like Causation and Perfection and Justice and Truth and come up with what we may choose to call the Absolute, over against which to demand the centrality of the cross for the knowledge of God stands as an offence against human reason. Nevertheless St Paul does not relent. 'Far be it from me', he wrote, 'to glory except in the cross of our Lord Jesus Christ', which does not call for an unreasonable religion, nor for the abandonment of the exercise of reason in religious thought, but the crucifixion is the starting point for a true knowledge of the nature of God and is at the heart of all that follows.

Let me elaborate—we must start with the cross of Christ and we must never leave it out, otherwise we shall find ourselves with a god of our own making and not with the real God. What this means in practice is that we begin our Christian life with gratitude. The characteristics are

106

relief, peace of mind, perhaps joy even, with singing sometimes occupying a spontaneous place. A man or woman who knows nothing of this,
even in a muted form, has never started the genuine Christian life for it is
a religion rooted in grace not in human effort, not even the effort or work
of faith, for faith is response to what God in Christ has done, it is saying
'yes' to the Word of the Cross. The response may come with Hallelujahs,
hand-clapping and tambourines, or it may not; temperament governs
these outward manifestations and they are not important. The essential
is in heart and mind to make the cross of our Lord Jesus Christ central
and to refrain from glorying in our own moral achievement and works of
charity, be they never so commendable, but they are useless to commend
us to God.

All this is true and indispensable as a beginning but there is more to be
said. The cross of Christ has a continuing part to play in the Christian
life. That life can properly be called *the Way of the cross*. What this
means is that self-centredness has to go, and this is hard, for we are born
with it, it is natural to us and the struggle to get free from it can almost
seem like a crucifixion. Even so, struggle is not the way of success. We
cannot simply shake it off. We shall only *grow away* from self-
centredness, if ever we do, by shifting our eyes off ourselves and in
communion with the crucified Christ discover the power of the risen
Lord. So St Paul's personal confession, 'I am crucified with Christ:
nevertheless I live; yet not I, but Christ liveth in me' (Galatians 2.20).

3 THE CRUCIFIXION DRAMA

And now something else. St Paul said we are to 'glory in the cross of our
Lord Jesus Christ'. Does this mean glorying in the *drama* of the crucifixion? Make no mistake, it is a most moving drama, even a tragic drama.
As such it can be enjoyed. Tragedy on the stage has always provided one
of the most powerful sources of entertainment. For reasons which must
lie deep within the human psyche it has a strange appeal, possibly
because we sense that a great part of human existence is a sorrowful
business. For this and other reasons, the story of the crucifixion does not
fail to attract attention. A few days ago I listened to a cassette recording
of Handel's *Messiah*. I was stirred by its strength and buoyancy but
when the contralto solo 'He was despised and rejected, a man of sorrows
and acquainted with grief' was sung I was almost overcome with the

tragic beauty of it, so gripped that there were tears on my cheeks; and, this is the significant point, I played it over again! I think I am a fairly normal human being, but apparently I *enjoyed* this sorrowful drama. The story of the crucifixion can play this part in religion so that Holy Week, Maundy Thursday, Good Friday and the ceremonies that have become associated with the events of these days, replaying the Passion story, are powerfully captivating, and in that sense enjoyed. Artistic enjoyment certainly need not be the end of the experience but if it is, then the outcome will be a gloomy religion. It is as unbalanced as the forced happy religion likely to follow when little but the forgiveness of sins is presented as the outcome of the crucifixion. Yes, it is right and proper for the Christian to tread the *via dolorosa* with Jesus in Holy Week, but not for the sake of the drama alone but to see again the full extent of the incarnation of Christ and how he faced pain, heartbreak, failure and rejection, even the apparent absence of God. We have not learned of Christ if our discipleship comes to a halt at the so-called triumphal entry into Jerusalem or with the reconciliation with God which the crucifixion undoubtedly achieved, but the 'Stations of the Cross' will not profit unless we stand before each one ready to learn, and not simply to enjoy a mood of sadness.

4 WHERE WE ARE TEMPTED TO GLORY

Once more we return to the text. 'But far be it from me to glory except in the cross of our Lord Jesus Christ, by which the world has been crucified to me, and I to the world.' These words occur in a letter in the New Testament in which Paul is blatantly blunt: 'You stupid Galatians! You must have been bewitched—before whose eyes Jesus Christ was openly displayed upon his cross! Answer me one question: did you receive the Spirit by keeping the law or by believing the gospel message? Can it be that you are so stupid? You started with the spiritual; do you now look to the material to make you perfect?' What was the trouble here? It was that some of the newly-won Christians in Galatia, having begun well enough by responding in faith unreservedly to the Christian Gospel of God's grace in Christ, went on to assert that observance of the Jewish law was *also* necessary, including the rite of entry, the distinctive badge of belonging to God's people, namely circumcision. Paul would have none of it. To say the least, it was racially and sexually divisive. Only one thing counts in the matter of our acceptance by God, nothing else. 'But far be it from me to glory except in the cross of our Lord Jesus Christ, by which the world has been crucified to me, and I to the world.'

And we shrug our shoulders and maybe look bored. Who cares about this historical situation, and one far away in Galatia in Asia Minor? But don't we slip into glorying about other things in our Christian discipleship as if they were basic and indispensable? Let me begin with myself. I am an Anglican, have been all my life, am committed to Anglicanism and love it. Have I never been guilty of assuming that this, of course, is the superior way? No one can be a real Christian unless he/she is an Anglican! To which St Paul would shout—nonsense! And you? You are a Presbyterian, a Roman Catholic, a Baptist, a Fundamentalist, a Liberal, a Charismatic. To all of us comes the basic challenge to say with St Paul, 'But far be it from me to glory except in the cross of our Lord Jesus Christ, by which the world has been crucified to me, and I to the world'. There is no call here to rub out our differences and abandon our allegiances, but if anything stands in the way of the cross of Christ, the one absolute essential for Christian discipleship, it must go. This is the test. This is where we come to the parting of the ways as to what is and what is not Christian—the cross of our Lord Jesus Christ.

23

OUR CRUCIFIED HIGH PRIEST

For it was fitting that we should have such a high priest, holy, blameless, unstained, separated from sinners, exalted above the heavens. He has no need, like those high priests, to offer sacrifices daily, first for his own sins and then for those of the people; he did this once for all when he offered up himself.

HEBREWS 7.26, 27 (RSV)

I bring to your notice a descriptive title of Christ which I think will probably be quite unfamiliar, if not strange to you unless you happen to be something of a student of the New Testament. The title Lord, Master, Teacher, Healer applied to Jesus will come readily to your mind, but not the title I am about to expound; indeed it is rare in the New Testament, occupying no place in the gospels and none in the writings of St Paul, but it does occur over and over again in one book, the epistle to the Hebrews, indeed is the basic theme of that book. It is Christ as our high priest. This is the title I must expound with reference to the crucifixion or this series of sermons will be open to serious criticism. Christ was crucified as our high priest.

The word 'priest' is emotive. It suggests a domineering ministry. Talk about priests in Northern Ireland and you will know what I mean. And to some extent strong reaction would be forthcoming in many parts of Scotland. In Eire the word would be taken 'lying down'. Priests are accepted there as part of life. In England we speak of 'clergymen', generally, though the words 'parish priest' have in recent years acquired a certain popular use, referring to a clergyman whose ministry is in a parish. The Book of Common Prayer generally refers to the 'Minister' though the word 'Priest' does occur where it is necessary to differentiate the minister from a deacon. In general it has to be said that the word 'priest' cannot be considered without reference to the Catholic/Protestant divide in the Church and this in itself tends to make it an emotive word though perhaps less so than formerly. In the light of all this however it does sound a little strange at first to call Christ our Great High

Priest, but he is this in one book of the New Testament, the epistle to the Hebrews. Listen to my text again, 'For it was fitting that we should have such a high priest, holy, blameless, unstained, separated from sinners, exalted above the heavens. He has no need, like those high priests, to offer sacrifices daily, first for his own sins and then for those of the people; he did this once for all when he offered up himself.' The reference is to the crucifixion and to Christ our crucified high priest.

1 THE WORK OF A PRIEST

Now the fundamental work of a priest, and this includes a parish priest, is to help people have access to God. I do not mean that without a priest this is impossible, though that position has been maintained by some strict Church people, I mean the priest is there with the people to open a door for them on to an experience of God for themselves. Let me give an illustration. I have used it elsewhere but it is the simplest, and for me the most authentic I know. At the age of eighteen I came to London as a student. I visited the sights of London as far as my limited opportunities and money would allow. I visited the National Gallery. Entrance was free. I knew nothing of art. There were no art galleries in the East Coast town from which I came, so I 'did' the National Gallery in about half an hour, only stopping occasionally to look for a few moments at some great battle scene or a portrait of some famous person I thought I knew. Then some three or four years later I happened to see in a bookshop—I was always scrounging round second-hand bookshops—a little hardback volume priced at five shillings (25p) called *The Observer's Book of Painting and Graphic Art*, fully illustrated. I bought it and studied it, and have to say that it opened the door for me on to a completely new and wonderful world. It gave me access to an experience of which I knew nothing. It was 'my priest' to something which hitherto was quite beyond me. Yes, it was simple, ludicrously simple in comparison with the great works there are on this massive subject, but it gave me a start and since then I have visited quite a few of the most famous galleries in Europe with at least some understanding and much appreciation.

The responsibility of the priest is to open the door for ordinary people into an experience of God. He may have many qualifications, some impressive: a double first at Oxford, a splendid singing voice, an athletic figure, 'film star' features, an easy manner with all sorts of people; and in

111

some circumstances these may turn out to be assets. But without two basic qualifications he will not be able to open the door to the experience of God for men and women, he will not give them access to 'the peace of God which passes all understanding'. He must have close sympathy with people as they are, not what he would like them to be, and wherever they are, and (let me stress this), whoever they are. This means sharing their joys and sorrows because he knows them from the inside; and secondly he must be a person of sacrifice.

2 JESUS THE PRIEST

I come then to ask my question. Was Jesus a priest in this sense? Does he qualify to be called a priest? Take my two points. Did he not open the door to give those he met an experience of God? Was not the very meeting of him such? How much more so when he spoke to men and women, healed them, touched them, yes, and on occasions grieved with them, cried with them, and sat down to joyous meals with them. People called him the friend of sinners, some in anger because they wished to find fault. And did not Jesus stand in with people? Had not his hands been dirtied and his feet worn with long journeys? Did he not know the feel of physical hunger and heartfelt sorrow? Listen to this from the epistle to the Hebrews: 'Seeing then that we have a great high priest who has passed through the heavens, Jesus, the Son of God, let us hold fast our profession. For we have not an high priest which cannot be touched with the feeling of our infirmities; but was in all points tempted like as we are, yet without sin. Let us therefore come boldly unto the throne of grace, that we may obtain mercy, and find grace to help in the time of need' (Hebrews 4.14–16 AV). And then this in the next chapter: 'Thou art a priest for ever after the order of Melchisedec. Who in the days of his flesh, when he had offered up prayers and supplications with strong crying and tears unto him that was able to save him from death, and was heard in that he feared; though he were a Son, yet learned he obedience by the things which he suffered' (5.6–8). Can there be any doubt that Jesus was a true priest? Read the gospels and you will see how close he was to people as they are. To which I cannot refrain from adding this comment, we shall not know the *Christ of faith* as he is unless we familiarize ourselves with the *historical Jesus*.

112

3 A PRIEST MUST SACRIFICE

And now the second qualification. A priest must sacrifice. In the old Hebrew economy priests had to belong to the tribe of Levi. There was what was called the Levitical priesthood, and the duty of the priests was to offer sacrifices, animal sacrifices for the sins of the people. And once a year, dressed in special garments, and with elaborate ceremony, the high priest alone entered the Holy of Holies to offer special sacrifices for the sins of the nation. No place, no ceremony, no day was more sacred than this. How then could Jesus be a high priest? He was not of the tribe of Levi but of Judah; this alone would seem to place him outside the range of possibility. And what sacrifices could he offer for the sins of the people? And where could he offer them? These were the questions which tormented the Jewish Christians to whom this letter called 'to the Hebrews' in the New Testament was addressed. How was the writer to answer them?

He answered them in the words of my text: 'For it was fitting that we should have such a high priest, holy, blameless, unstained, separated from sinners, exalted above the heavens. He has no need, like those high priests, to offer sacrifices daily, first for his own sins and then for those of the people; he did this once for all when he offered up himself.' The crucifixion was *the completion of his life of sacrifice*. It was a stainless, a sinless sacrifice, the sacrifice of a human life not the life of an animal. There was nothing more that could be done in the way of sacrifice. Jesus on the cross accomplished it all, anything else would be pathetically less, pathetically inadequate. There is a 'once-for-all-ness' about the crucifixion which is of the essence of the Christian Gospel. Let me quote this time from the First Eucharistic Prayer from the Order for Holy Communion Rite A, Alternative Service Book. 'Therefore, heavenly Father, we remember his offering of himself made once for all upon the cross, and proclaim his mighty resurrection and glorious ascension. As we look for his coming in glory, we celebrate with this bread and this cup his one perfect sacrifice. Accept through him, our great high priest, this our sacrifice of thanks and praise. . . .'

Need I say more? Jesus is our great high priest who made the one perfect sacrifice of himself in the crucifixion. So he is both *the priest and the victim* in his sacrificial act. I know there are some Christians who speak of the priest making the sacrifice in the Mass, placing much emphasis on the words of Jesus at the Last Supper, 'This *do* in remembrance of me'. There is a deep divide here. We must recognize this and be patient with it, behind it is a long history. Perhaps in recent ecclesiastical discussions some progress may be in process of being made, how the opposing views can be brought closer and Christ's one perfect sacrifice be made inclusive of whatever sacrifices we make as we carry out his command, 'Do this in remembrance of me'.

As I was thinking about the whole subject of Jesus as our crucified High Priest my eye lit on this verse in St Mark's version of the crucifixion narrative: 'The passers-by hurled abuse at him: "Aha!" they cried, wagging their heads, "you would pull the temple down, would you, and build it in three days? Come down from the cross and save yourself!" So too the *chief priests* and lawyers jested with one another: "He saved others", they said, "but he cannot save himself. Let the Messiah, the king of Israel, come down now from the cross. If we see that we shall believe." Even those who were crucified with him taunted him' (Mark 15.29–32 NEB).

O, if only some one could have approached those priests, 'chief priests', they are called, standing there, tapped them on the shoulder and said, 'Look there is the real high priest, over there, on that cross, which you have erected . . .'

There is nothing else to say, is there? Jesus is our crucified high priest.

24

A NEW SONG

Then I looked, and I heard around the throne and the living creatures and the elders the voice of many angels, numbering myriads of myriads and thousands of thousands, saying with a loud voice, 'Worthy is the Lamb who was slain, to receive power and wealth and wisdom and might and honour and glory and blessing!' And I heard every creature in heaven and on earth and under the earth and in the sea, and all therein, saying, 'To him who sits upon the throne and to the Lamb be blessing and honour and glory and might for ever and ever!' And the four living creatures said, 'Amen!' and the elders fell down and worshipped.

REVELATION 5.11–14 (RSV)

I read in the newspaper a few days ago that one of the choristers of Westminster Abbey, having sung there for 27 years, and reached the age of 60, has been asked to retire, and to put the matter lightly, 'he doesn't like the idea at all'. The experts however affirm that after that age a man's voice loses its quality. Well, if he isn't up to the standard required by the Abbey I hope he will go on singing, I hope he will go on singing in church, perhaps some other church though maybe not as grand as the Abbey. Singing in churches there must be, the best singing that is possible, and if our singing with the passage of time becomes somewhat croaky, then croak we must. This is my point. The Christian Church is not thoroughly Christian if it has no singing.

1 THE SONG

My text today from the last book of the Bible, the Revelation, tells of the new song that is sung in heaven and provides the words. There was a huge choir, myriads and myriads and thousands and thousands of angels, and this was the keynote of their anthem, 'Worthy is the Lamb who was slain, to receive power and wealth and wisdom and might and honour and glory and blessing'. And then the roar of the 'Amen' affirming the acclamation. What an anthem! What singing! And what a message! 'Worthy is the Lamb who was slain.' And you ask, where did John the author of the Revelation see that vast assembly singing and hear those striking words? In some marvellous church, shrine or temple? The answer is no, he had this vision and heard this singing in his mind where he laboured in a slate mine fifteen hours a day and seven days a week on the island of Patmos off the coast of Asia Minor; or if not there then some forced labour camp where he was chained for confessing the faith of Christ crucified.

2 THE LAMB

Listen to the words again of this new song. 'Worthy is the Lamb who was slain.' Who is this? It is Jesus Christ of course, Jesus Christ crucified, the lamb figure of speech taken from that impressive fifty-third chapter of the book of the prophet Isaiah in the Old Testament: 'He was oppressed, and he was afflicted, yet he opened not his mouth: he is brought as a lamb to the slaughter, and as a sheep before her shearers is dumb, so he openeth not his mouth'. And if you have ever sung in choirs as I have (though not after I was 60!) you will not be able to hear these words without the mighty music of Handel's *Messiah* ringing in your ears complete with the Amen Chorus. Jesus the Lamb of God is the recurrent theme of this book in the Bible, Jesus who was crucified. The word 'lamb' connects with the all-pervading sacrificial system of the Old Testament, the means by which the sins of God's people were done away. So purpose is introduced into the crucifixion of Christ. He did not simply happen to get caught, condemned and crucified. Maybe so it might seem to people for whom God plays no significant part in their thinking, but in reality the crucifixion was in God's purpose and plan for the redemption of the world. Lambs were often slain in the culture as portrayed in the Old Testament, especially on the great festivals like the Passover. Jesus was the Lamb of God crucified at the very time of the Passover Festival in AD 29 (or thereabouts) so that as the epistle to the Hebrews in the New Testament declares there is no more need of these continual sacrifices. He was offered once and for all.

Purpose and plan, I repeat, are wrapped up in this one pregnant description of Christ as the Lamb of God who takes away the sins of the world. What depths of mystery are brought to our attention by this! What understanding of the crucifixion far beyond it as a mere historical incident in the procuratorship of Pontius Pilate! And then in the thirteenth chapter of the Revelation there occurs this almost mind-boggling sentence, 'the Lamb that hath been slain from the foundation of the world'. God was not acting sacrificially for the world only from the time of the crucifixion, he has always been acting so since the world began and will be till the end of time. The crucifixion points to the activity of God always, activity on behalf of his people, activity on behalf of his world.

No, the Book of Revelation is not easy to understand, some parts of it are not easy to accept from the Christian angle for they sound so vindictive, but here and there are lights which in a flash illuminate our whole perspective. One such is this phrase 'the Lamb of God', the theme of the new song sung by the angels, and I hope repeated by us, with or without choirs in our churches. O Lamb of God that taketh away the sins of the world. *Agnus Dei qui tollit peccata mundi*. This is the Church's proper song. This is why we sing anything at all in our churches. The crucifixion is the root cause.

Is not this astonishing! A murderous act become the cause of our singing! And we go on telling the story of the crucifixion. We must go on telling it. It is the Church's basic story crowned with Easter Day and the knowledge of the Risen Christ and the fellowship of his Spirit. I make no apologies for devoting a whole series of sermons to the crucifixion taking trouble to try and make what happened (so far as we know) vivid to our imaginations, for only so will it live for us, and unless Christ lives for us, no matter how 'sound or unsound' our doctrine about him may be, that for which he came, suffered, died and rose again will be of scant spiritual profit.

3 THE THRONE OF GOD

We must not however stay over-long with the crucifixion; the book of Revelation does not stay with it. The new song that is sung is about the Lamb of God *on the throne with God*. Let us not be so wooden as to smile at the imagery—a Lamb on the throne! See instead how daring is all this. Do not overlook when this was written. It was the time when Domitian was on the throne of the Roman empire and emperor worship was the order of the day. Because of this and because of John's refusal to bow the knee he was in chains on the island of Patmos. What in effect John was saying in his book was that Domitian's day would end. Mighty monarch though he might seem to be, upheld by the mighty Roman legions, he would not forever reign. There will come a time when Christ will rule the hearts of men and women, ten thousand times ten thousand men and women, myriads of myriads and 'he shall reign for ever and ever'. Did this look likely from the dust-laden crevices of those hideous slate mines where he was hidden? Does it look likely today? Such is the daring Christian faith, so easily ridiculed, so frequently mocked, but there can be no other final hope.

I must make one final observation. The Jews were strictly, even fiercely monotheistic. There is one God only, one divine Being only on the throne. How then comes it that in the lifetime of a single generation there is seen to be Another on the throne? 'To him that sits on the throne *and to the Lamb*' wrote John in the Revelation. What an extraordinary impression Jesus of Nazareth must have had that these words could come to be written! 'They worship God and a crucified carpenter' was how the early Christians came to be lampooned by their contemporaries. But these critics were right in this—Jesus was worshipped as divine. He was worshipped as the Son of God; and this is the point for us to note in these sermons, the crucifixion on Skull Hill did not degrade him, it came to elevate him. The Lamb of God reigns with God. He is Christ the King of glory. And we repeat, 'Even so come Lord Jesus'.

So we look back in this series of sermons from the vantage point of the crucifixion to the foundation of the world—'the Lamb slain from the foundation of the world' (Revelation 13.8) and to his coming again as the ultimate ruler of the world he has redeemed, as the Scripture put it, 'by his blood'. The cross stands in the middle of time looking backwards and forward for it is timeless. Let us not pass it by regardless. Let us not grow used to it. Let us keep it central in our Churches and in our Christian discipleship. And if it does not make us sing or want to sing, let us go on contemplating it till we do.